Mona Siddiqui is Professor of Islamic Studies and Public Understanding at the University of Glasgow. She is a Fellow of the Royal Society of Edinburgh and the Royal Society of Arts. She has published in the areas of classical Islamic law and Muslim theology.

HOW TO READ

Available now

Forthcoming

HOW TO READ

THE QUR'AN

MONA SIDDIQUI

Granta Books
London

Granta Publications, 2/3 Hanover Yard, Noel Road, London N1 8BE

First published in Great Britain by Granta Books 2007

A CIP catalogue record for this book
is available from the British Library.

ISBN 978-1-86207-945-8

1 3 5 7 9 10 8 6 4 2

Typeset by M Rules

Printed in the UK by CPI Bookmarque, Croydon, CR0 4TD

CONTENTS

SERIES EDITOR'S FOREWORD

How am I to read *How to Read*?

This series is based on a very simple, but novel idea. Most beginners' guides to great thinkers and writers offer either potted biography or condensed summaries of their major works, or perhaps even both. *How to Read*, by contrast, brings the reader face-to-face with the writing itself in the company of an expert guide. Its starting point is that in order to get close to what a writer is all about, you have to get close to the words they actually use and be shown how to read those words.

Every book in the series is in a way a masterclass in reading. Each author has selected ten or so short extracts from a writer's work and looks at them in detail as a way of revealing their central ideas and thereby opening doors onto a whole world of thought. Sometimes these extracts are arranged chronologically to give a sense of a thinker's development over time, sometimes not. The books are not merely compilations of a thinker's most famous passages, their 'greatest hits', but rather they offer a series of clues or keys that will enable readers to go on and make discoveries of their own. In addition to the texts and readings, each book provides a short biographical chronology and suggestions for further reading, internet resources, and so on. The books in the *How to Read* series don't claim to tell you all you need to know about Freud, Nietzsche and Darwin, or indeed Shakespeare and the Marquis de Sade, but they do offer the best starting point for further exploration.

Unlike the available second-hand versions of the minds that have shaped our intellectual, cultural, religious, political and scientific landscape, *How to Read* offers a refreshing set of first-hand encounters with those minds. Our hope is that these books will, by turn, instruct, intrigue, embolden, encourage and delight.

Simon Critchley
New School for Social Research, New York

INTRODUCTION

Writing a book on the Qur'an is a challenge and a privilege. It is a challenge because one starts with the question – how can one ever do justice to a book which is believed by Muslims to be the direct word of God? It is a privilege because I follow in the footsteps of eminent Qur'an scholars who have paved the groundwork for so much of the critical thinking around one of the most widely read, revered and recited books in the world.

In writing this book as a British Muslim, I am keenly aware of how I read and use the Qur'an as a book of divine guidance and inspiration. I am also aware that along with the Bible, the Qur'an has been one of the most powerful books in human history. The influence of the book is global, with over one billion Muslims in the world who regard the Qur'an as God's last revelation. Over the last few decades the Qur'an has come under increasing scrutiny both by the Muslim and non-Muslim world, the media and the academy. Modernity challenges those who follow an ancient text for moral and social guidance. How can scripture stay relevant and how can it provide solutions in a world of complex moralities?

Many Muslims refute the suggestion that modern readings of the Qur'an can be problematic. Their position is simple: it is only by obedience to the Qur'an that society can live properly. Yet this is a reductionist view of the text itself. The power of the book emerges as the faithful read and interpret it in the light of new and changing situations. The Qur'an, like all scripture, is open to contextualized changes in understanding and interpretation. Furthermore, recent critical and literary tools of investigative scholarship have raised new questions. Exactly how was the Qur'an revealed and how was it received? How did the Qur'an take shape as a 'book'?

In this work, I have understood the Qur'an within Muslim belief: that its origins lie in God himself and that the Qur'an acts as a focus for the faithful, their central source of divine inspiration and guidance in all matters of life. Yet the process of revelation is undeniably complex: when the divine word becomes the written word, it is appropriated by human beings. Human beings read and understand in their own contexts and with the legacy of inherited tradition. When that legacy is divorced from today's social and moral concerns, how should interpretation continue?

Contemporary ethical approaches to pluralism, diversity, medical advancement, social justice and civic duty, challenge the traditional ways in which the Muslim scriptures have been understood. Scriptural verses do not solve complex moral problems. There are no definitive solutions to many of the issues raised by human rights' discourse and the globalization of society. As institutional religion faces a struggle to survive, which voice of authority and guidance should the believer follow? The purpose of this book is to let the reader enter the Qur'an, to understand its power and influence for Muslim societies and to show how believers practise and often struggle with certain directives. It is also my own journey, a reflection of the faith I follow as a believer and a faith I question as a scholar. Although there have always been and will continue to be competing and contested claims on the history and meaning of the text, modernity has thrown these claims into sharper focus. Pluralism, women's rights, political determinism and freedom of conscience are universal discourses in which the Muslim world also has a legitimate voice.

Note on Terms

I use both the terms God and Allah on different occasions in this book. At times, I have found it disconcerting to hear both Muslims and non-Muslims go to great lengths to attribute significance to one over the other. For me they remain different names for the same being. When referring to the prophet Muhammad, I have also used both designations, the 'Prophet' and 'Muhammad'. In Muslim practice though, which for ease of reading I have here left out, reverence and love of the Prophet means that any reference to Muhammad is generally followed by the phrase 'Peace be upon him.'

THE BOOK AS GUIDANCE

Sura al-Baqarah (The Cow) Q2:1–7
This is the Book. In it is guidance without doubt for those who fear God. Those who believe in the Unseen, are steadfast in prayer and spend out of what we have provided for them and who believe in the Revelation sent to you and sent before your time and believe strongly in the Hereafter. They are on a true guidance from their Lord and it is these who will prosper. As for those who reject faith, it is the same for them whether you warn them or don't warn them; they will not believe. Allah has set a seal on their hearts and on their hearing and on their eyes is a veil; great is the penalty they (will) incur.

Islam is a world religion, practised in almost every part of the world in diverse languages and within diverse cultures. Within this diversity one book is central to Muslim belief and worship. This book is the Qur'an (also Koran), for Muslims the direct word of God and the most recent of the major world scriptures to appear in human history. Although Muslims have been living in the West for centuries now, there has been little understanding by most non-Muslims of the place the Qur'an holds in the social, political and cultural history of Islam, nor its centrality in the religious practice of the believer. Western scholarship of the Qur'an has developed considerably over the last few years and serious scholarly contributions have focused on the historical contexts of the Qur'an, the processes leading to the formation and compilation of the book in Arabic and how the Qur'an retained its central position in Muslim thought and culture. But scholarly works are generally read only by those in the academy. For most, the Qur'an is seen through the prism of an individual's understanding of religion in general, and in particular their views on Islam and the Qur'an in the Western world. This had led to various interpretations about the place of the Qur'an in Muslim life and thought.

While religion and its place in society has resurfaced to major debate in the last few years, Islam, more than any other religion, has been the recipient of the world's focus, both politically and within the media. Islam has dipped in and out of the public gaze ever since the crisis over Salman Rushdie's *The Satanic Verses* in 1989, and common statements such as 'Islam is the most misunderstood faith', or 'Islam is demonized' and the 'West and Islamophobia' have become an increasing part of political and global discourse. No more so than since the attacks on the World Trade Center towers in New York on 11 September 2001, which for some were seen as direct conflict between the Muslim world and the West. Since the bombings on the London transport system in July 2005, the rhetoric around the 'war on terror' has reached fever pitch. These bombings were interpreted not just as the aggressive face of home-grown militancy amongst young people who practised the Muslim faith, but more disturbing evidence of a failed multiculturalism. The question on the lips of many has been, 'Why have so many in the Muslim communities failed to integrate in wider society and why are they so against the West?' In these debates, many turn to the Qur'an for answers but for some it is regarded as the root of the problem. If radicalism, terrorism, social and legal inequalities for women, and religious intolerance are features of Muslim societies, then surely there is something in the scripture of these communities which lends itself to this kind of thinking? How can Muslims interpret the Qur'an as a book of mercy and justice when the consequences of this interpretation appear medieval, outdated and antithetical to modern democratic values? These kinds of questions provoke emotional, often defensive reactions and Muslims argue that this perception of Islam is simplistic. They claim that it is the misunderstanding of the Qur'anic message by some Muslims which leads to inequalities and oppression prevalent in many Muslim societies. The non-Muslim world should search for a deeper understanding of the Qur'an, and not judge the faith by those oppressive cultural practices in the Muslim world.

Inherent in this kind of criticism and defence is a naive assumption that scripture alone is responsible for how Islam has developed and how it is practised in society. It overlooks the way that religious tradition stems from its own social and cultural milieu, in its own historical context. Scripture and its interpretations did not emerge in cultural and social vacuums. The Qur'an was revealed in a historical context. The awareness of changing contexts is fundamental to understanding the eternal value and relevance of scriptural texts. If the Qur'an is, as it claims, 'a straight path in which there is no doubt', the book must be able to offer guidance of eternal value and application, its verses unchanging but open to a variety of interpretations, receptive to exploration as society itself changes.

How the modern world and the modern Muslim stay engaged with a seventh-century text is the task of the believer when he reads and tries to understand the Qur'an. The challenge is huge, for Islam did not simply bring about a quiet submission to God. God's revelation in the Qur'an brought forth a whole new religion, a new civilization with empires which flourished throughout the word, known for their richness and sophistication. When Muslims turn to the Qur'an today, they are aware that the Qur'an and the spread of Islam changed not only the course of Arabian history but world history. As Daniel Brown wrote in a recent introductory book on Islam:

> One of the great puzzles of early Islamic history is the sheer unlikeliness of what actually happened. A thoughtful Arab living in the Arabian Peninsula, a short time before the conquests would have had every reason to laugh out loud at the suggestion that Arabs would soon be world rulers, representatives of a new universal faith, and purveyors of a vibrant civilisation.[1]

These largely Arab, desert roots provide the social and moral context for the emergence of Islam. Islam, like Christianity, is in its origin a non-Western religion. Its roots are in the Hijaz, the Arabian peninsula, which in the sixth century was largely desert, although agriculture existed in the settled communities in the south and camel herding was one of the main occupations of the nomads (Bedouins). Traditional accounts maintain that the Hijaz was becoming a prosperous trade spot, and that Mecca was a thriving centre of commerce, but recent scholarship casts doubt on the value of this trade. Rather than luxury goods such as spices, merchants were trading in more humble items such as leather, leather goods and dates.[2] The commercial sophistication of Mecca may have been less than previously thought.

Monotheism existed in the peninsula prior to Islam. Aside from Christian and Jewish communities in the region, there were *hanifs*, believers who were neither Jewish nor Christian. The word 'hanif' refers to one who has turned to monotheism because inclining towards God is part of man's natural disposition. The Qur'an refers to Abraham as a hanif implying that Abraham reached monotheism through individual insight (Q6:79). Mainly, though, Arab groups worshipped idols and spirits. Social ethics were based on tribal loyalty and group solidarity which also led to intertribal warfare. The pre-Islamic period of Islam, commonly known as the *jahiliyya*, is often referred to as the period which stands in contrast to everything Islam brought. The word occurs four times in the Qur'an to distinguish the period before God's revelation. It evokes a state of ignorance in which darkness and moral decadence are implicit. God's revelation brought about a revolutionary change – this new message changed the moral climate of the Arabian landscape from what existed before the coming of 'guidance'.

The Islamic message of the Qur'an points to a new way of thinking about this world and about life beyond this world. First and foremost, the Islamic message rejects the multiple gods which the Arab communities created and worshipped, for the sake of the One True God whom they couldn't see but who was the Creator of all, a revolutionary idea for the polytheists. The one true God was the message of the first revelation made to Muhammad in the small cave in Mount Hira in 610 CE.

The word Qur'an derives from the Arabic verb *qar'a*, 'to read aloud'. Qur'an literally means 'recitations' or 'the reciting'.[3] For Muslims, the Qur'an is the word of God revealed to his last prophet, Muhammad (*c.*570–632 CE), through the medium of the angel Gabriel, known in the Qur'an as Jibril.

All accounts of Muhammad's life originate from Ibn Ishaq, a scholar in Medina famous for writing his first full biography. Known as the *Sirat Rasul Allah* (Biography of the Messenger of God), it was written about a century after Muhammad's death and provides the first coherent outline of Muhammad's life. Ibn Ishaq's work comes to us through the writings of a ninth-century scholar, Ibn Hisham, who heavily edited Ibn Ishaq's original work.[4] In this biography, it is said that Muhammad's father died around six months before his birth and that he was brought up by his grandfather Abd al-Muttalib of the Banu Hashim clan of the tribe of Quraysh. At the age of six, his mother Amina also died. Now an orphan, Muhammad was raised by his uncle Abu Talib. Muhammad had gained a reputation of reliability and honesty and in 591 CE this attracted a proposal of marriage from Khadijah, a wealthy widow, who was involved in the camel-caravan trade and was some fifteen years his senior. Khadijah supported Muhammad fully and was the first to accept the message which became known as Islam.

In 610 CE, when Muhammad was around forty years old, he regularly withdrew to the outskirts of Mecca to meditate. During one of his mediations in the cave of Hira, the angel Gabriel came to him and the first revelation took place. Muhammad describes this experience:

> The angel came to him and asked him to read. The Prophet replied, 'I do not know how to read.' The Prophet added,

'The angel caught me and pressed me so hard that I could
not bear it any more. He then released me and again asked
me to read and I replied, 'I don't know how to read.'
Thereupon he caught me again and pressed me a second
time till I could not bear it any more. He then released me
and again asked me to read, but again I replied, 'I do not
know how to read.' Thereupon, he caught me for the third
time and pressed me, and then released me and said,
'Read in the name of your Lord, who created, created man
from a clot.'[5]

The first revelation descended during the month of Ramadan,
which subsequently became the Muslim holy month of fasting. From that moment on for the rest of his life, between 610
and 632 CE, Muhammad received revelations. They were oral
in nature – words spoken to him or words which he found
in his heart and then uttered. The Prophet described this
phenomenon:

Messenger of God, how does the revelation come to you?
The messenger of God replied, Sometimes it comes like the
ringing of a bell: it is the hardest on me. Then it passes
from me after I have grasped what it said. Sometimes the
angel appears to me like a man. He speaks to me and I
grasp what he says.[6]

These revelations were transmitted orally to Muhammad's
followers, who memorized them or wrote them on palm
branches, stones, animal skin or papyrus. On the death of
Muhammad in 632 CE, copies of various verses were in existence but there was no 'copy' of the Qur'an as a compiled
book. While Muhammad was alive, there had been no real

concern for preserving his words in any collected form. Indeed there is no evidence that he viewed his messengerhood as dependent upon his bringing forth a physical book. His successor, Abu Bakr, had some reservations about collecting the Qur'an in its entirety without Muhammad's authority. The process of compiling a written version of the Qur'an began formally during the lifetime of the third caliph, who was both the religious and community leader, Uthman b. Affan (*d*.656). He commissioned the Medinan Zayd b. Thabit, who had been one of Muhammad's scribes, to collate an official written copy. This written text would be based upon oral and written records of Muhammad's utterances. Within twenty years of Muhammad's death, the complete *suras* or chapters had been collected and the Qur'an as a 'book' came into being as a defined corpus of writing. This book, known as the 'Uthmanic codex' or 'Uthmanic mushaf', was used as the model for all subsequent copies of the Qur'an distributed throughout the lands and regions under the expanding Muslim rule. It was the official text, declared authentic and closed, so that no longer would anyone be able to add or subtract any word. The Uthmanic mushaf sealed the Qur'an and established it as written text rather than oral recitations for ever.

It is said that Uthman kept one copy in Medina and sent other copies to Kufa, Damascus and Basra, commanding that any other extant copies be destroyed. Despite Uthman's commands, some survived with slight variations. Furthermore, Uthman's codex was preserved in consonantal form without vowels, in accordance with the custom of writing Arabic. Scholars disagree as to exactly when and how the Qur'an became scriptio plena, a fully vowelled text, although the process by which Uthman's text became the accepted version took almost two centuries. During that time, Qur'anic orthography contained within it both consonants and vowels, which affirmed a 'correct' reading of the Qur'an and which has been the model for all Qur'ans. It is generally acknowledged that despite the variations, the original Arabic text has remained remarkably uniform in all extant editions from the time of the Uthmanic codex. For many Muslims, the Qur'an's historical preservation is a sign of divine intervention itself. God has taken it upon himself to preserve the Qur'an in its original form, safe from human corruption. Reading the Qur'an in this original form is reading God's words directly and is believed to incur blessings. This is why even though translations of the Qur'an are now available in almost every major language, the Qur'an continues to be read and recited in Arabic.

An Arabic Qur'an is opened from right to left in accordance with the way Arabic is written. It is not a thick book. The whole of the Qur'an is contained in 114 suras, literally 'rows' or chapters. The first sura in every Qur'an is al-Fatiha, 'The Opening', a prayer recited in Muslim worship. However, it is disputed whether sura al-Fatiha is the first revelation Muhammad received. The suras are arranged in order from the longest to the shortest and most have a title reflecting a theme within the sura. Each sura, apart from the sura of 'Repentance' (Q9), begins with the phrase of *basmala*, 'In the name of God, the Merciful, the Compassionate'. Some claim that the basmala was inserted later, others that it was part of the original revelation from God. Muslims speak this phrase before all sorts of activities, from eating to going on a journey. A note at the head of each sura designates whether the sura was revealed at either Mecca or Medina, the city where Muhammad settled in 632 CE. Twenty-nine of the chapters of the Qur'an are preceded by a letter or a sequence of letters, the meanings of which are not always clear, but which are also considered part of the original revelation.

For most Muslims, the pages of the Qur'an encapsulate God's latest and greatest revelation, final in its wisdom and guidance. The transmission of the Qur'an and its compilation are not issues which exercise the minds of most Muslims. The shift from the oral discourse to the written word does not present a challenge to the absolute veracity of the Qur'an. They refer to the divine status of the Qur'an as a miracle beyond imitation, which God has taken upon himself to preserve from human corruption. Even the sources which explain how the Qur'an was compiled under Uthman's rule are of little significance. What is important is that God is the author of the Qur'an, it is God's last revelation, divine in origin, unchanged and eternal; the Qur'an's words, its composition and order, are all exactly how the Qur'an was meant to be. It was God's wish that the content, the form and the ordering of the suras in the Qur'an are exactly as we now have it.

Yet the timelessness of the Qur'an juxtaposes itself against the particular historical context of Muhammad's life. Many of the verses are revealed in relation to Muhammad's life and the questions he was asked by both the believing and sceptical communities around him. The constant appellation 'say' in the Qur'an signifies a response to a moral, social, personal or theological question or explanation which Muhammad is seeking. Muhammad's own experiences create the context and substance for the Qur'an. Thus, Muhammad's life and person are linked inextricably with the Qur'anic message and tone. When people accepted that Muhammad was receiving a divine message, his role as the recipient of the Qur'an elevated him to the status of a Prophet, the embodiment of the ideal man. The Qur'an frequently commands, 'Obey God and his messenger.' The basic confessional creed of the Muslim is 'There is no god but God (Allah) and Muhammad is His Messenger'. This confirms the oneness of God with the messengerhood of Muhammad, both central to the book's genesis and its central message; God is the speaker in the Qur'an and Muhammad is the recipient of this message. Later Muslim commentators developed a whole literature in which superhuman qualities were ascribed to Muhammad, who in essence was predisposed to convey the 'straight path' to the Meccan community. For Muslims, revelation and prophecy form the dual basis for understanding God's will.

To look at the Qur'an as scripture alone – a book to be read, recited or memorized – only partially reflects its esteem and influence amongst Muslims. In its relationship to Muhammad, the Qur'an contains the fundamentals of man's relationship with God and man's relationship with others. It is a book with one overriding moral thesis – man's destiny lies with God and man is lost if he thinks otherwise. Reading the Qur'an is a constant reminder of this relationship. There is a saying of Muhammad that 'The most excellent form of devotion among my people is reciting the Qur'an'. For the vast majority of Muslims then the Qur'an is not simply a book of faith, it points to a divine choice. God chose to intervene in human history for the final time and through Muhammad, the Qur'an was born as a final reminder of the 'right path'.

Despite the transformative power of the Qur'an in the eyes of many believers, reading and understanding the Qur'an has never been a simple matter; the Muslim intellectual traditions bear testimony to that. Although the text of the original Arabic may have remained unchanged, the Qur'an has not remained a static text; it has always been understood and interpreted in a variety of ways. One has only to note the different Muslim cultures around the world to perceive the diversity of religious expression, even though the Qur'an remains a unifying force. Muslims everywhere read the same verses of the Qur'an but understand those readings in their personal, historical and social contexts. Yet despite different interpretations, the modern world challenges the Muslim understanding of the Qur'an. Modernity challenges all faiths and Islam particularly is criticized as arcane and even medieval in its thinking, especially in relation to certain human rights issues. Many Muslim scholars maintain that the socio-legal verses of the Qur'an must be seen in their historical context, where what was commanded was relevant to that particular time and is no longer applicable today. This is one of the many debates which aim to realize the more ethical and generous dimension of the Qur'anic message. It is unfortunate that there is a growing tendency among many Muslims to attempt to find only one meaning, only one solution to all of life's problems.

2

READING AS REVELATION

Sura al-'Alaq (The Clot) Q96
Read in the name of your Lord who created, created man
out of a mere clot of blood. Read and thy Lord is most
bountiful. He who taught the use of the pen, taught man
that which he knew not. But man transgresses all boundaries for he looks upon himself as self-sufficient. Verily to
thy Lord is the return of all. Do you see the one who forbids
the worshipper when he turns to pray? Do you see if he is on
the road of guidance or enjoins righteousness? Do you see if
he denies (truth) and turns away? Does he not know that
God sees? Let him be aware! If he desists not, we will drag
him by the forelock, a lying sinful forelock! Then let him
call for help to his council. We will call on the angels of
punishment to deal with him. Do not heed him: But bow
down in adoration and bring yourself the closer to God.

Although there is some dispute over whether two other suras
are the first words revealed to Muhammad – al-Fatiha (The
Opening) and al-Mudaththir (The Covered One) – the above
sura, which is placed 96th in the Qur'an, is generally regarded

as Muhammad's first experience of divine revelation. The Qur'an speaks directly to Muhammad, strongly conveying the sense of another voice, the voice of God. Muhammad is commanded to 'read' that there is a bountiful God who exists, who has created man out of a blood clot and who has taught man all that he knows: the Lord of mankind. This God demands our obedience and worship and it is to this God that we will all return. Although the rhythm of the verse is largely lost in the English translation, it is an extremely powerful sura, especially the first few lines of the sura. A contemporary scholar, İbrahim Özdemir, states that 'reading' here means a 'completely new way of looking at the world. At the very beginning it is taught that God, as the Sustainer and Creator, gives existence and meaning to everything else . . . all reality should be seen and read with this point of view in mind.'[7]

The verses of the ninety-sixth sura illuminate how man's being and fate are tied up with his relation to God. Man is created from a blood clot, a nod here towards the biology of human creation.[8] Man was created unknowing until God gave him knowledge, until God breathed into him his own breath. This breath imbues in man a noble dignity above the rest of creation. The all-powerful and omniscient God gave man knowledge so that man would thirst for knowledge of God. Yet, man in his arrogance does not turn to God and there are those who stop others from the true worship of God; these people will be punished for their wrongs.

Revelation or 'reading' is necessary to bring back man to God, the God who created man and the God to whom all of humanity will return. For Muslims, the Qur'an is God's last revelatory intervention in human history. God speaks and reveals as and when he chooses. Though God has spoken to man in different ways throughout human history, his final revelation in the Qur'an emphasizes the unicity of God. Revelation in Islam is conceptualized within a fundamental theological paradox: God reveals through the Qur'an yet God remains completely unknowable. In reading the Qur'an, the believer encounters God but God remains transcendent, beyond human understanding. Compare this to the status of Jesus in Christianity where God reveals himself through his son; God becomes man in order to communicate with humanity. Islam and Christianity have not been short of their respective theological debates about the nature of man's relationship with God, but at the heart of this debate is a fundamental agreement that we need divine revelation to understand the mystery of life. While man may think he is self-sufficient, that there is no being greater than him, different revelations throughout human history direct us back to that which lies beyond us – God. For his part, God's interest is the well-being and prosperity of man and he wishes to remain close to his creation. This is why God has sent throughout the course of history reminders of who he is and the message of a 'straight path'. That said, the Qur'an makes it clear that God does not communicate with man directly:

> It is not fitting for a man that God should speak to him except by *wahy* [inspiration] or from behind a veil or by sending of a messenger to reveal with Allah's permission what God wills; for He is exalted and Wise. And thus have We revealed to you, the spirit of Our command. You did not know before what the book is nor what faith is but We have made it [the Qur'an] a light whereby We guide whomsoever We will of our servants and indeed, you guide people to the straight path.

Muslims see the Qur'an as the direct words of God to man; it is not a work of human authorship. The words, mediated through Gabriel, are from God and God's will is always present in the revelatory process. 'Jibril brings revelation to your heart by Allah's will' (Q2:97). Gabriel (Jibril), the mediator of the entire Qur'an, is traditionally an angel but at times he is also referred to as a 'holy spirit'. The term 'wahy' refers to God guiding or inspiring something or someone. In another sura, 'Your Lord sent "wahy" to the bee to build its hives in hills, on trees and in the houses of men' (Q16:68). Nature depends on a higher being to realize its own ways. Wahy contains within it the sense of a revelatory process prior to the act of recitation itself.

Although Muslim belief understands revelation in its simplest sense as the words 'revealed' to Muhammad through Jibril, the Qur'an uses various words to refer to the process of revelation. When I hear Christian friends talk about the 'mystery' of the Trinity, I think of the parallel in Islam, the 'mystery' of the Qur'an. Both are central to their faiths but the precise nature of both has posed huge challenges to the faithful. The Qur'an tells us that the earthly Qur'an, the collection of verses into a book, has a prior existence. A complete Qur'an is preserved on a heavenly tablet (*lawh mahfouz*) in the realm of eternity. The Qur'an mentions this in Q85:22: 'Indeed this is a glorious Qur'an, inscribed in a Tablet Preserved.' Classical scholars of the Qur'an claim that it descended in three stages. In the first stage, it came from God to the 'preserved tablet', a tablet which is also referred to as Umm al-Kitab (Mother of the Book). For Muslims, this is an original heavenly book, the archetype in which all earthly revelations including the Qur'an and also the Jewish and Christian scriptures have their origin. Second, the Qur'an was sent from the highest heaven to the lowest heaven; third, it was sent or 'revealed' via Jibril to Muhammad over a period of 22 years.[9] For most Muslims, then, the earthly Qur'an, bound between two covers, is an accurate transcript of the eternal 'Preserved Tablet'. The speech of God is the same as that written in the physical book of God.

Accounts of the process and duration of revelation differ in the Qur'an. According to two verses, the Qur'an was revealed at a specific time: 'Ramadhan is the month in which the Qur'an was sent down as a guide to mankind, also signs for guidance and judgement' (Q2:185) and the much recited, 'We sent the revelation from high on the night of Power' (Q97:1), again understood as one of the last few nights during the month of Ramadhan. These verses point to a singular moment when the Qur'an was revealed in its entirety while many other verses speak about the gradual nature of revelation. For instance, 'those who deny say, "Why was the Qur'an not revealed to him as a single utterance?" It is thus, so that We may strengthen your heart thereby and We have rehearsed it to you gradually in stages'(Q25:32). Also, 'And it is a Qur'an which We have divided into sections in order that you may recite it to humankind at intervals. And we have revealed it in stages' (Q17:106). Early Muslim scholars tried to reconcile both the gradual and the one-time view. For some, the Qur'an was revealed as a 'single utterance' when it descended into the lower heaven, but it was still revealed to Muhammad gradually. They had established the tradition of *asbab al-nuzul* or 'occasions of revelation'. This interpretation had grown around the need to understand many of the Qur'anic verses in their historical context, as direct responses to various episodes in Muhammad's life. Much of the content of the earthly Qur'an was seen to be rooted in the immediate issues and dilemmas which Muhammad faced during the last twenty-three years of his life. The ethical guiding principles in Muslim life originate mainly in the life of the Prophet. Revelation is thus both historically bound and yet remains ahistorical.

The Qur'an itself uses different words to reflect the concept of revelation. It consistently refers to itself as a book, although it was not in any book form during the period of revelation. The Qur'an was unwritten at the time of revelation, yet it refers to itself as a piece of writing. The Qur'an refers to itself as 'Book of God' (*kitab allah*), revelation (*tanzil/wahy*), 'wise book' (*kitab hakim*), 'mercy' (*rahma*), 'guidance' (*hudan*), 'distinguisher between right and wrong' (*furqan*). There are many others and the Qur'an scholar Aliza Shnizer says, 'The sheer number of titles, descriptions and metaphors used by the Qur'an to describe its own nature as a divine book revealed by God himself, is quite unique'.[10] The different ways the Qur'an names itself underlines that the Qur'an is a new guide – the new expression of God's will for the salvation of man. But its titles also implicitly refer back to other texts. God has revealed himself in different ways throughout history and the essential message of the Qur'anic revelation is the same. The Qur'an is a reminder to man to return to the worship of the one true and just God, the same message of all the previous revelations.

The Qur'an is a God-centred book and the unicity of God, known in Islam as *tawhid*, is its central message. Urging the Meccan community to believe in the oneness of God was for Muhammad his biggest challenge. It meant demanding not only that the Meccan idolators physically destroy their existing idols, but that all other religious communities adhere to the Islamic truth and never associate another being with God.

God has been revealed to humanity before in different ways, through different books. In Christianity, revelation came in the form of incarnation – in Jesus, God became man; in Judaism, the Ten Commandments on Mount Sinai are divine revelation. The Qur'anic narrative constantly alludes to past revelations, prophets and scriptures to enunciate its moral message. Stories about Noah, Abraham, Jesus and Moses appear throughout the Qur'an. But if the reader expects a coherent narrative about most of these prophets and the events of their life, he may end up feeling a little frustrated. With very few exceptions the Qur'an is neither chronological nor thematic in the way it presents its material. The suras relate the stories in an often disjointed manner. This is partly because the Qur'anic style is not based on story-telling; rather it uses narrative clips to illustrate moral points. Take the stories about the pre-Islamic Arab communities of Ad and Thamud: these stories provide no historical information, instead they illustrate how communities were destroyed for disobeying God.

Without revelation, man can exist but it will be a meaningless life because it will not be directed to God and the afterlife. Believing in God's punishment or reward in the Hereafter is a necessary corollary of believing in God. In Muslim belief, the Qur'an and everything it talks about are signs of God's presence and omnipotence in the world. The Qur'an does not only talk about God but is the sign of the existence of God. Arabic has been chosen as the medium of revelation, to facilitate its understanding to an Arab messenger: 'We have sent it down an Arabic Qur'an so that you may heed' (Q12:2) and also:

> Had we sent this as a Qur'an in a foreign language, they would have said, 'Why are its verses not explained in detail? What a foreign language and its messenger an Arab!

Say, for those who believe it is a guide and a healing and
for those who do not believe, there is deafness in their
ears and a blindness in their eyes. (Q41:44)

That Islam spread with an Arabic Qur'an gave the Arabic
language a unique place in Islamic civilization. It was the language of revelation for practising Muslims. Even today, most
ordinary Muslim families will teach their children Qur'anic
Arabic before they learn to read anything else. Whether
taught at home or in a *madrasah* (a religious school), starting
one's education with the Qur'an is the Muslim ideal. In many
cultures, families and friends celebrate the beginning and
finishing of the Qur'an. Children and adults may not always
understand the Arabic but the original text is read for the
purpose of prayer and worship. Many non-Arabic-speaking
Muslims usually read a translation of the Qur'an alongside the
Arabic. For some, the ultimate act of piety is to memorize the
whole Qur'an over a number of years, an achievement worthy
of honour and respect in the community.

The earthly Qur'an is a constant reminder of the Divine
and of the intimate tie between God and man. God has given
man one last opportunity to turn towards him. The Qur'an
occupies a unique place in the lives of Muslims. It is read,
recited and heard not only to derive meaning from but for lis-
tening to the beauty of the Arabic language. God's revelation
has come not in the form of a dry, logical treatise to frighten
the community into believing in him. God's revelation has
descended in beautiful words, in rhythmic prose and steeped
in the message of divine mercy.

3

GOD'S ONENESS

Sura al-An'am (The Cattle) Q6:95–9; Sura al-Baqarah (The Cow) Q2:255

It is Allah who causes the seed-grain and the date-stone to sprout. He causes the living to come forth from the dead and He is the one to cause the dead to come forth from the living. That is Allah, so then how are you deluded from the truth? It is he that breaks the day and makes the night for rest and the sun and moon for the reckoning. Such is his judgement, the Exalted in power and the Omniscient. It is he who makes the stars for you so that you may guide yourselves with their help through the dark spaces of land and sea. Indeed we detail our signs for people who know. It is he who produced you from a single soul and then a resting place and a repository. We detail our signs for people who understand. It is he who sends down rain from the skies. With it we produce vegetation of all kinds.

Alone is God, there is no God but Him, the Alive, the Sustainer; neither sleep nor slumber overtakes Him. To Him belongs whatever is in the heavens and on the earth – who can then intercede with Him except whom He permits? He

knows what is before them and what is behind them, while
they encompass none of his knowledge, except what he
permits. His Throne envelops the heavens and the earth
and their preservation fatigues Him not – He is the High,
the Great.

The Qur'an is a God-centred text; the 'I' or 'we' in the Qur'an
is God speaking to man. God is king, God is judge and God is
mercy. Through the act of creation, God expresses all three of
these attributes. The Qur'an gives ninety-nine names for God
to express his diverse attributes, but all are premised on the
fundamental belief that God is One and God is essentially
unknowable. Thirty times, the Qur'an repeats, 'There is no
God but Him,' and it has multiple ways of relating the oneness,
the munificence and mercy of God. The God of the Qur'an
guards his unity fiercely; it is an uncompromising monotheism.
It is God who has given us life, it is God who will cause us to
die and then raise us again from death. Nothing is impossible
for God, for it is he who gives everything its place and order.
In return for his blessings, he desires our worship and acknowl-
edgement that there is no other like him.

When we observe the beauty and symmetry in nature, this
is itself a sign of divine mercy, for nature's order has been created for man to reflect upon and thereby comprehend God.
God is *al-rahman*, the Merciful one. This mercy is the overriding attribute of God even when we disobey, when we are
ungrateful or when we do wrong. God's mercy and forgiving
nature is mentioned over 500 times in various ways in the
Qur'an. One of God's names is *al-Wadud*, the loving one.
Though the theme of divine love is not as strong in the
Qur'an as the theme of divine mercy, God wishes to be close
to his creation. God loves in response to human devotion and

worship and the Qur'an's emphasis on repentance is a
reminder to the believer of the forgiving God. While it is true
that the Qur'an is replete with exhortations to man to observe
nature, to turn to God, to desist from denial of God and dis-
belief (*kufr*) so as to avoid the punishment of the Hereafter, the
Qur'an also says that God will forgive man all of his sins:

> Say, O my servants who have transgressed against their
> souls. Do not transgress against the mercy of Allah for Allah
> forgives all sins. He is oft-giving, most merciful. (Q39:53)

Even when man has committed the biggest transgression of
elevating anything else to the same level as God, the possibil-
ity of forgiveness is there:

> Allah does not forgive associating anything with Him. But
> he forgives other than that as he wills. But the one who
> associates with Allah has indeed strayed far away. (Q4:116)

Some of the most poignant descriptions of God are in the
literature of the *hadith*, the sayings attributed to Muhammad
which are not in the Qur'an. The following hadith describes
God's love and forgiveness of man:

> O son of Adam, so long as you shall call upon me, I shall
> forgive you for what you have done and I shall not mind. O
> son of Adam, were your sins to reach the clouds of the sky
> and were you then to ask forgiveness of me I would forgive
> you. O son of Adam, were you to come to me with sins
> nearly as great as the earth and were you then to face me,
> ascribing no partner to me, I would bring you forgiveness
> nearly as great as the earth.

The mercy of God is linked to God's nearness to us, His awareness of our needs and our prayers:

> My servant does not draw near to me with anything more loved by me than the religious duties I have imposed upon him, and my servant continues to draw near to me with supererogatory works so that I shall love him. When I love him, I am the hearing with which he hears, his seeing with which he sees, his hand with which he strikes, and his foot with which he walks. Were he to ask [something] of me, I would surely give it to him; and were he to ask me for refuge, I would surely grant him it.[11]

And then there is the Qur'anic verse, 'It was We who created man and we know what his soul whispers to him for we are nearer to him than his jugular vein' (Q50:16). God is near to man but remains beyond man's imagination. Although the Qur'an speaks of God's transcendence, it also speaks of God's hands, God's face, God sitting on a throne. Such anthropomorphic descriptions of God have been subject to various interpretations in the early period of Islam. What does it mean to say God speaks or God hears or God sees? What faculties does God have to do such things? The task of the philosophers and the theologians was to reconcile a God who could be understood through human images yet one whose essence remained unknowable.

As Islamic civilization spread and flourished, intellectual debates around these issues grew. The Mu'tazilites were one of the most prominent intellectual and theological movements of the eight and ninth centuries who emphasized God's justice and unity. They argued that the oneness of the eternal God is absolute and God did not resemble his creation in any way. A logical consequence of this unity was that everything apart from God was created by God. This included the Qur'an, which was not eternal but the created speech of God. The opposing idea from the Asharis was that the Qur'an was the uncreated, eternal speech of God, and that the Qur'an on earth, in the form of a book, is the earthly manifestation of God's eternal word. This opposing idea won the battle and established itself as the orthodox belief among Muslims.

The Qur'an states that the absolute oneness of God can never be compromised. The message of the one creator, who has sent previous revelations to humanity as a sign of his mercy, binds Islam to other monotheistic traditions, especially Judaism and Christianity. But although the Qur'an mentions the prior revelations which produced the Jewish and Christian communities, several tensions remain between the faiths. Islam shares with Judaism a belief in one indivisible God, but it parts ways with Christianity in its doctrine of the Trinity. The Muslim God is merciful but transcendent while the Christian God is loving and immanent. The Muslim God sends revelation and his mercy but remains untouched by this process, whereas the Christian God is intimately bound with the life of his creatures and their suffering is his suffering. The Muslim God promises salvation for those who turn to him, while the Christian God sacrifices his son to save the whole of mankind. Such comparisons reveal deep theological differences between Islam and Christianity, so that many people from each religion claim that the Muslim and the Christian Gods are not the same being. The Abrahamic link between Islam and Christianity creates a bond between the two faiths, but both faiths express monotheism in different ways. In recent years, many Muslims and Christians have reopened such discussions in an attempt to narrow the distance between Muslim and Christian views of monotheism. From the Muslim perspective, the relatively crude perception of the Christian Trinity as three gods has gradually been replaced by a deeper appreciation of the complexities of the Christian understanding of three distinct persons in one essence. This is a difficult challenge for many Muslims, because the Trinity suggests the divisibility of God. It has been a fundamental and contentious issue in Christian–Muslim polemics, mainly because the Qur'an specifically alludes to the Christian belief:

> They disbelieve who say Allah is one of three for there is no god except one God. If they don't desist from what they are saying, a grievous punishment will befall those who disbelieve (Q5:73).

> Say, He is Allah the One, Allah the Eternal and Absolute. He does not beget nor is he begotten and there is none like Him (Q:112).

The following verse claims that Jesus, the only prophet who will be brought back to earth before the Day of Judgement, will himself be asked:

> O Jesus son of Mary, did you say to people, take me and my mother for two gods besides Allah? He will say, Glory to you, never could I say what I had no right to say. Had I said such a thing, you would have known it. You know what is in my heart though I do not know what is in yours. For you know too well all that is hidden. Never did I say to them anything other than what you commanded me to say, 'Worship Allah, my lord and your Lord,' and I was a witness

over them whilst I dwelt among them. When you took me
up, you were a watcher over them, and you are a witness to
all things. (Q5:116–17)

Jesus, a revered prophet in Islam but not regarded as divine,
will be questioned on the Day of Judgement; no one will be
exempt on that day from what they taught their followers or
what they learnt from the prophets who were sent to them.

Many Jews, Christians and Muslims refer to the common
thread in their faiths, which can be traced back to the
Abrahamic tradition. Abraham, who lived in Arabia, is a foun-
dational figure in the Qur'an. He is referred to as a hanif, a
man who practised a kind of primordial monotheism in
opposition to the idolatory rife in his time. As well as
Abraham, the Qur'an also echoes the message of all the previous prophets of the Near East. In the phrase 'confirming
what went before'(Q6:92), the Qur'an refers to the previous
revelations received by both Moses and Jesus. Here, too, the
truth of the oneness of God, his prophets, righteous conduct
and belief in the Day of Judgement was delivered to the
prophets, and each prophet in turn confirmed God's sovereignty throughout history.

God's oneness implies that everything in creation is sub-
servient to him. He is the judge whom we will face on the
Day of Judgement, when our earthly deeds and actions are
weighed up. At the end of this life will begin another life,
'God made the heavens and earth in truth so that each soul
could be rewarded for what it earned' (Q45:22). Our own
mortality lies in contrast to God's infinity, 'All that dwells
upon the earth is perishing; yet still abides the face of your
Lord, majestic, splendid' (Q55:27). Muslims affirm God's
presence in their life in the constant remembrance of his

name. The invocation of God is generally encapsulated in
dhikr, the Qur'anic word meaning remembering or mention-
ing. For the Sufis or mystics, dhikr became the central feature
of their worship, and meditation on God's name is practised in
more formal rhythmic patterns by the individual or in a
group. Remembering God is a fundamental characteristic of
Muslim life. In ritual worship such as daily *salat* (formal
prayers), God's name is mentioned in multiple ways. It is
common to say 'Praise be to God' after sneezing, the words
'May God reward you' instead of thank you, or 'As God
wishes' when witnessing or hearing good news about someone. These phrases are not an extra act of piety but normal
speech, part of everyday conversation. In this way God's name
is kept alive in people's hearts and minds. In many Muslim
households, it is also common to see plates, ceramics, frames
and wall-hangings inscribed with the words 'Allah' and
'Muhammad' in Arabic calligraphy. These protect the owner
from evil and are a constant reminder that God is present in
the lives of the faithful.

The Qur'an itself brings us closest to describing the beauty
and mystery of God in the following sura:

> Allah is the Light of the heavens and the earth. The para-
> ble of His light is as if there were a niche and within it a
> lamp. The lamp enclosed in glass, the glass as if it were a
> brilliant star, lit from a blessed tree, an olive neither of the
> East nor of the West, whose oil is almost luminous, though
> fire scarce touched it. Light upon Light; Allah guides whom
> he will to his light. (Q24:35)

In this poetic image, God remains radiant, omniscient and yet
elusive. He is the light which guides, but like light remains

beyond form. Light cannot be captured. It is illuminating yet without definition. Contrast this with the physical and brutal image of Christ on the cross, a God whose blood and death epitomizes self-sacrifice. This image evokes real anguish and pain.

Monotheism has come to us in different ways throughout history but the Qur'an insists that the message of all revealed religions has been that of faith in God and an afterlife. Beyond that the laws and dictates of these religions have been different, indicating a divine will to offer varying paths to people at different stages of history. This perspective needs to be emphasized in contemporary society, where the resurgence of a more conservative and intolerant Islam argues for the rejection of the multiple visions of Muslim societies. What is even more disturbing is the growing discourse in some Muslim communities which claims to state with absolute conviction what is God's exact will on a number of issues. These dogmatic views are based on a selection of Qur'anic verses and they range from issues of dress, marriage, gender relations to politics. Such discourse leads to a narrow and fearful Islam, one stripped of an inner generosity and inquiry. It is imperative that Islam is not reduced to dogma alone and that Muslims accept that apart from belief in the oneness of God and the messengerhood of Muhammad, other aspects of Muslim life and thought have remained open to challenge and change throughout the history of the Muslim world. It was the believer's passion for trying to understand how and why God continued to reveal which led to the outpouring of the post-Qur'anic intellectual heritage in philosophy, theology and law. Within these traditions, there lies deep thought combined with a certain humility, that in the end, although the believer can try to understand, ultimately God and his will remain unknowable.

4

PROPHECY AS MERCY

Sura al-Mu'minin (The Believers) Q23:44
Then We sent Our messengers in succession. Every time there came to a people their messenger, they accused him of falsehood . . . We sent Moses and his brother Aaron, with our signs and manifest Authority. To Pharaoh and his chiefs but they behaved insolently; they were an arrogant people. They said 'shall we believe in two men like ourselves? And their people are subject to us!' So they rejected them and they became of those who were destroyed. And we gave Moses the Book in order that they might receive guidance. And we made the son of Mary and his mother as a sign.

The reaction to the satirical cartoons of the prophet Muhammad first published in the best-selling Danish newspaper *Jyllands-Posten* on 30 September 2005 throws into sharp relief Muhammad's status in the Muslim world.[12] Twelve caricatures of Muhammad were printed in the paper to accompany an editorial criticizing self-censorship in the Danish media. Two in particular caused offence. One showed Muhammad standing on a cloud holding back a line of smouldering suicide bombers trying to get to heaven. Muhammad is saying, 'Stop, stop, we have run out of virgins' (a reference to the sura which talks of the reward of heavenly virgins for the righteous). Another shows Muhammad as a terrorist, carrying a lit bomb on his head in the shape of a turban decorated with the Muslim creed. The fury and anger of hundreds of Muslims throughout the world led to protests, a ban on Danish goods, the recall of ambassadors, arrests and even several deaths.

Whatever one thinks of the reaction, it became apparent to even those who know little about Islam that the prophet Muhammad holds a very sacred place in the Muslim faith. Indeed, Islam's central character is Muhammad. He is described by a number of epithets such as *rasul allah* (Messenger of God), *nabi karim* (Blessed Prophet) and *habib Allah* (God's beloved), all of which reflect his nearness to God. Muhammad is not just one prophet in a long line of prophets but the Prophet, the last chosen prophet and the recipient of the last divine revelation. He is referred to in the Qur'an as the '*khatam al-nabiyyun*' (seal of prophets), after whom there will come no more messengers or prophets.

Medieval Muslim thinkers, dwelling on this phrase, 'seal of prophecy', concluded that Islam was the most perfect and final form of an evolution in religion. This belief is echoed by modernist thinkers such as the late Pakistani–born Fazlur Rahman, who wrote:

Several Muslim modernists have held passionately that with and through Islam and its revealed book, man has reached rational maturity and there is no need for further Revelations. In view of the fact that man is still plagued by moral confusion, however, and that his moral sense has not

> kept pace with his advance in knowledge, in order to be
> consistent and meaningful, this argument must add that
> man's moral maturity is conditional upon his constantly
> seeking guidance from the divine books, especially the
> Qur'an, and that man has not become mature in the sense
> that he can dispense with divine guidance. It must further
> be held that an adequate understanding of divine guidance
> does not depend any more upon 'chosen' personalities but
> has become a collective function.[13]

Rahman adds that since Islam, there have been other claims
to prophecy but no 'successful claimants'. As well as
Muhammad, the Qur'an mentions twenty-eight other persons
chosen by God to spread the message of unity and obedience,
although not all were given a scripture to accompany their
prophecy. Muhammad is a messenger in the historical line of
prophets such as Noah, Abraham, Moses, Jesus as well as those
not mentioned in the Bible, such as Hud Thamud and Shuaib,
prophets from Arabia. But Muhammad is not just chronologically the ultimate messenger; he embodies the universality of
prophecy. God has made a special covenant with previous
prophets including Noah, Abraham, Moses and Jesus, but
they were all prophets who were sent to their own nation
with the language of their people. Muhammad, however,
appears in certain Qur'anic passages to be a prophet whose
message was not just for the Arabs but was a universal message; his role was to be a mercy to all mankind (Q4:79).

For this reason, the Qur'an reflects both aspects of
Muhammad's prophecy; the mission to ensure that the message
of monotheism destroys polytheistic beliefs but also that Islam
prevails over all other religions (Q9:33). From the very first revelation, when Muhammad is told to recite, it is Muhammad's

role to spread the message he receives to his tribespeople, the Quraysh, and the rest of Meccan society. After his migration to Medina in 622 CE, Muhammad eventually establishes what Muslims consider a small Islamic state, the seeds of an empire that was to expand rapidly and make Islam a world religion.

Muhammad's role was twofold. Primarily, he is honoured as the recipient of God's final revelation. However, he also left his own sayings in the form of hadiths and the word sunna defined his personal practices and habits. Although sunna at the time conveyed a general sense of behaviour to be followed, when applied to the Prophet, it signified more specifically exemplary action and prophetic precedence. Muhammad's words and actions are known within the corpus of the sunna literature and are considered to be extremely authoritative in the lives of Muslims. Over the centuries Muslim belief increasingly venerated Muhammad and gradually established literary and legal discourses in which Muhammad's words and actions provided the basis and parameters for righteous behaviour for all Muslims for all time. Centuries of theological debates have considered the relationship between Muhammad as a person and his role as the Messenger of God. The central doctrine of prophethood states that infallibility is intrinsic to prophecy, for prophets carried, received and conveyed divine revelation. They had to be reliable and free from error and sin. If the Qur'an as God's last revelation was perfect in form and content, it had to be received by a prophet who was also perfect, sinless and worthy of receiving such a revelation. A story about Muhammad demonstrates his purity: one day, while Muhammad was tending sheep, two men dressed in white came upon him with a golden basin of snow. They opened his breast, took hold of his heart and stirred their hands inside. These men were angels who extracted a black speck from his heart and then cleansed his heart with the snow. In other words, Muhammad had been chosen and prepared to receive revelation from an early age.

The Qur'an's view is that prophets are always subject to doubt and ridicule by their respective communities. This creates not only a personal challenge for them but is also a test for their communities, who must recognize God in human prophets. The Egyptian pharaohs refused God because their own arrogance blinded them to the prophetic reality. Muhammad faced a similar fate. In the earliest response to Islam, various charges were levelled at Muhammad. He was accused of having written the Qur'an himself or borrowed from Jewish and Christian sources. Later Muslims replied that the Qur'an's reference to Muhammad as an unlettered prophet, meant that he was illiterate and incapable of producing such a work. Though there is some doubt as to whether Muhammad was completely illiterate, this assertion was helpful in Muslim polemics in defence of the Qur'an's divine origins. Early Christian polemics against the prophecy of Muhammad led Muslim scholars to define the miraculous nature of the Qur'an in the tenth century. Al-Rummani, a theologian and grammarian, argued that the Qur'an's unique style and literary merits could not possibly be of human origin. He found references to its quality in the Qur'an itself:

> Say, if the whole of mankind and jinns were to gather together to produce the like of this Qur'an they could not produce its like, even if they backed each other with support. (Q17:88)

Why God chooses people to convey his message through prophets is not explained in the Qur'an; it is simply accepted as the way a just God chooses to guide his creation to worship him. Prophets in the past have been rejected, accused of being soothsayers or forging lies, but despite the rejections they faced, God stood by them in their trials and persecutions:

> Mankind was one single community and Allah sent messengers with glad tidings and warnings; and with them He sent the Book in truth, to judge between people in matters in which they differed. (Q2:213)

> Do you think that you will enter paradise without trials as came to those who passed away before you? They met with suffering and adversity and were so shaken in spirit that even the messenger and those of faith who were with him cried, 'When will come the help of Allah? The help of Allah is near.' (Q2:214)

The Qur'an tells us that mankind was a 'single nation' (Q2:213) and theologians debated whether all people were followers of polytheistic faith before the advent of prophetic missions, or believers in the one God who then disagreed among themselves, and needed prophets to remind them of the primordial message. Many Muslim exegetes argued that the primordial religion of all people was Islam. Humans were Allah's servants, starting with Adam, considered the first Prophet. It is this primordial Islam which Abraham followed and which preceded both the Torah and the Gospels. These previous prophets were Muslims, a word which literally means 'one who surrenders'. Muhammad is a Muslim in the sense of 'surrendering himself' to God, 'Say, I have been commanded to serve God, purifying my religion for him and I have been

commanded to be the first of those who have become
Muslim' (Q39:11–12).

Muhammad did not leave only the Qur'an as guidance for
his community. He also left his own teachings and his own
practice, regarded as exemplary conduct to be emulated, the
basis of moral and ethical behaviour. Despite a chain of
prophets preceding Muhammad, they are in Muslim thinking
virtually eclipsed by the figure of Muhammad. His religious,
social, moral and political roles are the defining moments of
Muslim life. Muhammad's role was not just that of prophet
but also the ultimate authority on all matters for the emerging
Muslim community. The Qur'an says:

> You have indeed in the messenger of Allah, a beautiful
> pattern of conduct for anyone whose hope is in Allah and
> the Final Day and who remembers Allah much (Q33:21).

> Obey Allah and obey the Messenger and beware (Q5:92).

Muhammad's life and words are encapsulated in sunna, a word
which originally meant the practice of any community but
came to be associated with Prophetic precedent. The development of the Prophet's sunna was a gradual process for the
Muslim community and captured in reports and sayings
attributed to Muhammad which became known as hadith.
Hadith cover virtually every aspect of Muhammad's life and
sayings, attributed either to Muhammad or to his companions;
hadith are prophetic in origin not divine like the Qur'an.
They range from what Muhammad said or did in his battles
with Meccans, to business matters, to conducting relations
with people of other faiths, and relations with his wives, to
issues of piety and devotion to God:

An adulterer at the time he is committing illegal sexual intercourse is not a believer and a person at the time of drinking an alcoholic drink is not a believer, and a thief at the time of stealing is not a believer.

One should mention the name of Allah on starting to eat and one should eat with his right hand.

Yahay related to me from Malik from Salama ibn Safwan ibn Salama az-Zuraqi that Zayd ibn Talha ibn Rukana, who attributed it to the Prophet, said, The Messenger of Allah, may Allah bless him and grant him peace, said, 'Every religion has an innate character and the character of Islam is modesty.'

Whoever goes in the search for knowledge, engages himself in the cause of God till he returns home.

Although the large bulk of hadith are words attributed to Muhammad, uttered as his response to a question or event, many of the hadith qudsi give general moral directives:

Whosoever of you sees an evil, let him change it with his hand and if he is not able to do so, then with this tongue and if he is not able to do so, then with this heart and that is the weakest of faith.

None of you truly believes until he wishes for his brother what he wishes for himself.

The Prophet of God said, 'When God finished the creation, he wrote in his book which is there with him, above the throne, Indeed, my mercy overcomes my wrath.'[14]

The vast movement in hadith collection began only after Muhammad's death and with the spread of the Islamic empire. As Islamic civilization expanded politically and culturally, the need to find authority to regulate different cultural practices became paramount. Prophetic hadith guided the believers to right behaviour and the will of God. Some hadith specialists travelled far and wide to gather accurate information. To ensure that what was being attributed to Muhammad was authentic, it was imperative that the chain of transmission led back to him. A scholarly discipline was created to establish the authenticity of hadith. In an oral culture, where information passed from person to person and generation to generation, it was important to know that the people who were attributing words to Muhammad were of noble character and excellent memories. Hadith were divided into two parts, the '*isnad*', the chain of transmission, and the '*matn*', the actual content of the report. They were graded on the reliability of the chain of transmission. Collecting hadith, the raw material of traditional Islamic learning, was considered an extremely pious activity. The ability to discern reliable hadith from the weak and or forged hadith, was a pinnacle in the pursuit of knowledge amongst early Muslim scholars. This activity reached its zenith in the ninth century in the works of Muhammad ibn Isma'il al-Bukhari (*d*.870) and Muslim ibn al-Hajjaj (*d*.875). Their collections of hadith are considered the most authoritative compilations and are widely used by Muslims. Four other collections of Abu Dawud, al-Tirmidhi, al-Nasa'i and Ibn Maja have also attained canonical status. These written compilations constitute 'official' and 'closed' corpora like the Qur'anic corpus. Muslims now had access to two sets of official 'corpora', and for the most part Muslims have viewed the Qur'an and sunna as complimentary bodies of knowledge.

Theological inconsistencies emerging from these works are often ignored, partly because of the Qur'anic command to 'obey God and his prophet'. Most Muslims understand both the Qur'an and the hadith as part of the same revelatory process, where the boundaries between transcendent divine word and historic, prophetic action remain somewhat blurred.

Muhammad is regarded as the living example of the Qur'an, the embodiment of right behaviour. But the variant hadith on single issues, the length of time which lapsed between Muhammad's life and the subsequent hadith compilations, raise the fundamental question of their reliability; whether they are valid as historical data or reflections by generations of Muslims who could not possibly have known with any certainty what Muhammad said or did but wrote only what they believed.

These questions have troubled Muslims because much of the dogma of Islamic tradition has been based on the selective use of hadith citation. Hadith have assumed a quasi divine status and are highly influential in Muslim attitudes to many issues in life as well as giving rationale to certain institutional practices. Many would argue that hadith have been misused to keep women subjugated, to create societies where women have no public voice and to allow for the practice of certain inhumane forms of punishment.

The use of hadith in ordinary conversation amongst Muslims is nothing new. However, over the last two decades, there has been a growing tendency to cite hadith to justify all aspects of individual behaviour. The attempt to emulate Muhammad in all aspects of his life, whether in his relations with his wives to the clothes he wore, creates much controversy among Muslims. Very often, emulation is considered a pious activity even though there may be little concern for either spirit or context. It is for this reason that some Muslims called for the death of the editor during the *Jyllands-Posten* cartoon crisis. The caricature of Muhammad was in their eyes tantamount to blaspheming against him, and in Muhammad's time, blasphemy had on occasion merited the death penalty. In their view, Muhammad is sacred, and his actions and words are applicable for all time, relevant always for the believer.

The verses at the beginning of this chapter remind the faithful that prophecy throughout history had one fundamental purpose, to tell people of the one true God. Prophets have come and gone but only God remains. The Qur'an says:

> Muhammad is no more than a messenger. Many were the messengers that passed away before him. If he dies or were slain, will you then turn back on your heels? (Q3:144)

As God's final prophet, Muhammad's teaching remains the source of religious and moral behaviour for Muslims. However, this teaching must be seen within the overriding theme of the Qur'an – God's eternity and mercy. Though inspired and directed by God, he remains a voice responding to the historical exigencies of his time. If the purpose of the prophetic voice is to inspire moral and ethical frameworks for society, that voice must not be trapped in seventh-century Arabia, but be allowed to speak through humanity's changing circumstances; the message of divine mercy must never be forgotten. Prophetic practice and precedent is contained in a large body of written material which requires careful analysis and articulation for the modern world. Ethical paradigms can draw on the resources of the past but they must not insist on recreating that past.

5

MAN'S CREATION AND VOCATION

Sura al-Baqarah (The Cow) Q2:30–36
Behold, thy Lord said to the angels, 'I will create a
vicegerent on earth.' They said, 'Will you place therein one
who will make mischief and shed blood? Whilst we do celebrate your praises and glorify your holy name?' He said, 'I
know what you know not.' And he taught Adam the names
of all things, then he placed them before the angels and
said, 'Tell Me the names of these things if you are right.'
They said, 'Glory to you of knowledge, we have none save
what you have taught us; in truth it is you who are perfect in
knowledge and wisdom.' He said, 'Oh Adam, tell them their
names.' When he had told them their names, God said,
'Did I not tell you that I know the secrets of heaven and
earth, and I know what you reveal and what you conceal?'
And behold, 'we said to the angels: 'Bow down to Adam and
they bowed down: not so Iblis; he refused and was haughty:
he was of those who reject faith.' And we said, 'Oh Adam,
you and your wife dwell in the Garden and eat of the bountiful things therein as you will: but do not approach this tree
or you will be from the transgressors.' Then did Satan make

them slip from the Garden and get them out of the state in which they had been. And we said, 'get down all you people with enmity between yourselves. On earth will be your dwelling place and your means of livelihood for a time.'

In the Qur'anic story of man's creation, man is God's vice-gerent on this earth. Adam is fully aware of his creation and his dependency on his Creator. Within creation as a whole, it is man whom God has created for a special purpose. The above passage is less concerned with the biological processes of creation – no references to blood clots here – instead it focuses on man's intellectual and spiritual properties. God has predetermined that man have knowledge and this knowledge gives him a place at the centre of creation.

Adam is the first human being but news of his creation is not met with eagerness by God's pre-existing creatures. The angels question God about why he is creating a being that will cause bloodshed on earth. The divine response is: 'I know what you do not know.' (Early commentaries on the Qur'an attributed this bloodshed by man not to Adam but his descendants who do not follow God's law.) Then God tests the angels by asking them to name what is around them, but they do not have this knowledge and realize the error of their question. Adam knows the names and it is his knowledge of all things animate and inanimate which distinguishes him. The angels prostrate themselves in response to God's command and in recognition of Adam's superiority, except Iblis who refuses. Adam and his wife – who remains nameless in the Qur'an – are commanded by God to live in paradise. Then Adam, too, is tested. He is told to eat whatever he wishes but to stay away from a certain tree lest he transgress. Commentators differ as to the species of tree but the Qur'an refers to it as a tree of eternity (Q20:120). Adam is tempted by Iblis to eat from it, an action which is termed a *zalla*, a 'slip,' and both Adam and his partner are ejected from paradise.

This narrative has parallels with the Biblical creation story, but the Qur'anic events lead to a theological difference between the two traditions. Several suras tell and retell the story of Adam's expulsion from paradise and when all the disparate but related parts are considered together, the moral lies within Iblis's temptation of man and the consequences of this temptation for man and Iblis. Adam is not the main character of this narrative. Iblis's story begins when he disobeys God's request to acknowledge Adam:

> When God said to the angels, 'See I am about to make man from clay; when I have fashioned him and breathed my spirit into him, fall down bowing before him.' Then the angels bowed themselves all of them together, except Iblis for he was haughty and became one of the unbelievers. God said, 'Iblis, what prevented you from bowing yourself before what I have created with my hands? Are you haughty or are you one of the high and mighty ones?' He said, 'I am better than he. You have created me of fire and him you have created from clay.' Then God said, 'Then get yourself out of here for you are cursed! And my curse shall be on you till the Day of Judgement.' Iblis said, 'My Lord, give me respite till the day the dead are raised.' God said, 'You have been given respite till the day of the known time.' Iblis said, 'Then by Your power I will lead them all astray except your sincere servants amongst them.' God said, 'This is the Truth and the Truth I say that I will fill hell with you and those who follow you every one of them.'
> (Q38:71–85)

Iblis is expelled for his refusal to obey God's command and becomes known as the 'cursed satan'. This disobedience is a central feature of the Qur'anic creation story. He starts his work as the 'cursed satan' in leading Adam astray in the garden:

> But Satan whispered evil to him. He said, 'O Adam, shall I take you to the tree of eternity and to a kingdom that never decays? They both ate of the tree and so their nakedness appeared to them and they began to sew together leaves from paradise for their covering. Thus did Adam disobey his Lord and fall into error. But his Lord chose him; he turned to him and guided him rightly. (Q20:115–22)

These verses describe the aftermath of Iblis's expulsion from paradise and his resolve to ensure that Adam and the rest of humanity be expelled too. Despite God's reassurance that the paradisean state is enough for Adam and his wife, Adam falls victim to his desire for immortality. Not only has Adam broken an initial covenant he had with God, he also ignores God's warning about Iblis's sly and manipulative ways. The story of Adam's weakness is the story of human weakness in the face of temptation and greed. For this error, Adam and all of mankind lose the blissful state of paradise for ever. However, when the broken narrative is pieced together, the emphasis is on Iblis's decision to work against God's goodness. Adam is forgiven by God for his error but must now live with his wife on earth until an appointed time. Although Adam's wife is not held responsible for tempting Adam, Islamic exegetical works drawing largely on biblical sources known as *isra'iliyyat*, established Eve as a primary cause in Adam's 'slip'.[15]

Muslims understand Iblis in different ways: an evil being with an independent existence, or a personification of evil and part of the human condition; either way, his goal in life is to win loyalty and to lead people away from the worship of the one true God. To combat Iblis, Muslims begin many religious activities, including the reading of the Qur'an with the prayer, 'I seek refuge with Allah from the cursed shaytan.'

In the Qur'an's description of man's essential nature we find the most significant difference between the Qur'anic story and its biblical counterpart. In Islam, man's 'slip' remains a slip and not a sin. The Qur'anic account concentrates on the fall of Iblis rather than the fall of man. Adam's slip leads to his expulsion from paradise but Adam does not remain eternally damned; he is forgiven by God and must now live on earth and try to follow the right path. One could argue on the basis of the opening verses that when God speaks to the angels of Adam's vicegerency on earth, it is clear that Adam and his partner are destined for earth even before the transgression. The 'slip' leads to man's integration within the world of nature, where man assumes the particular role of custodian. God is merciful for he sends prophets and revelations. Only in following the right path defined through prophecy and revelation is there hope of salvation. In Christian doctrine, the original sin of Adam's fall taints mankind in its entirety. It is a sin so great that only through the coming and the death of Christ himself is man redeemed. Salvation through Christ is central to Christian theology whereas in Islam, the rhetoric of salvation is never the primary focus of theological debate. The Qur'an and God's mercy provide routes for the deliverance of mankind from damnation, and routes for success and prosperity. Human beings do not suffer from an ontological deficiency such as 'original sin'. Human beings are blessed with a 'sound nature', *fitra*, which enables them to make distinctions between right and wrong; salvation lies within us.

In forming man, God breathed into him his divine breath. Verses such as 'We created man in the best of forms' (Q95:4) and 'He fashioned you in the best of images' (Q40:64) have led to various theories on man's position and purpose in life. God's breath elevates man. He is endowed with an inherent dignity and God-like knowledge; he has a purpose distinct from the rest of creation. The status of *khilafat* means that Adam and his progeny are entrusted to look after the earth. This seems like a blessing but it is in fact a huge burden man has taken upon himself. The heavens and the earth had refused this burden and the Qur'an calls man 'foolish' for assuming this vocation (Q33:72). Yet, having accepted, the earth is in man's care and he can make use of her riches:

> It is We who have placed you with authority on earth and provided you therein with means for the fulfilment of your life. (Q7:10)

> Do you not see that God has subjected to you (for your use) all that is in the heavens and the earth and has made His bounties, both seen and unseen, flow to you in exceeding measure. (Q31:20)

Earth's natural laws, such as the setting of the sun, rising of the moon, recurring seasons and the coming of the harvest, are not only reflections of God's bounty but are also divine signs for man to reflect upon. They are not passive, they have their own reason and rhythm, and convey compelling stories in the narrative of creation. They each in their own way sing

God's praises and conform to the laws he has set for them. One could say that the Qur'an invites man to a spiritual, hermeneutical reading of the universe.

Muslim communities have revived the concept of man's stewardship of the earth, responding to growing ecological concerns around sustainable development and climate change. Stewardship as a divine mandate demands that we acknowledge other living beings on the planet and work to maintain a balance between the various resources at our disposal. In a world where ever-increasing concern for the environment is translated into safer social and global policies on ecological issues, Muslims are turning to the Qur'an and hadith to try and better understand man's relationship with nature and the environment. From the hadith, we learn that Muhammad encouraged the planting of trees, kindness to animals and prohibited the destruction of vegetation. The Qur'an teaches that the earth should not be pillaged for its resources, 'Waste not by excess for Allah does not love the wasters' (Q6:141). Although God can create and re-create the earth as he wills, man is not to subjugate the earth for short-term gain. Just as all nature glorifies God in its own way, so will this natural universe rise up on the Day of Judgement to hold man accountable:

> When the earth shall quake violently and the earth will bring forth its burdens and man shall say, 'What is happening to it?' On that day it shall tell its stories. (Q99:1–4)

The Qur'an is unique among other monotheistic religions in its ecological approach, conceiving of environmental concerns as divine will. Thomas Michel, a Jesuit scholar, considered the differing Christian and Muslim approaches:

> How many tales, how many complaints, covering so many centuries will the earth be able to tell, of contaminated seas, of polluted air, of lands made desolate through over-production and wartime destruction, of forests stripped, of animals killed unnecessarily for sport or for their furs, hide and tusks, of whole races of animals and plants wiped out through the indiscriminate use of pesticide and the dumping of industrial wastes, of its beauties disfigured and its treasures sacked, all in the name of greed masquerading as progress. The point is that humans will not go unpunished for the sins and misdeeds which they have committed against the earth. The Qur'an views earth as a creature of God which has an inalienable dignity which should be respected.[16]

In his social relations, in his dealings with those around him, in his stewardship of the earth, man can find meaning and purpose drawing him closer to God. As the Muslim philosopher and thinker Muhammad Iqbal said:

> No doubt, the immediate purpose of the Qur'an in this reflective observation of nature is to awaken in man the consciousness of that of which nature is regarded a symbol . . . to awaken in man the higher consciousness of his manifold relations with God and the universe.[17]

In his custodianship of earth, man is made aware of his own servility and God's omniscience. The relationship between man and God raises questions about divine omnipotence and human free will. Three approaches sit side by side in the Qur'an, not fully reconciled. First, everything happens by God's predestination; second, there is some cooperation

between God and man in human action and third, man himself is responsible for his actions. Some verses embrace all of
these perspectives:

> No soul can believe except by the will of God (Q10:100)
> Say the truth is from you lord; let him who will believe and
> let him who will reject but you shall not will except as God
> wills (Q81:29)

Free will is studied in *kalam* or *ilm al-kalam*, which techni-
cally means the 'science of discourse or words'. Islamic
theology, like other monotheistic traditions, never managed to
fully reconcile predestination with human freedom, although
different schools of thought grew up around the debate. After
the death of the Prophet in 632 CE Muslim theologians
explicated the faith for the believers and defined who was and
was not a Muslim. It concentrated on issues such as faith
and works, unity of God and the eternity of the Qur'an, and
freewill and predestination were also closely considered. These
debates created various theological schools in which Muslim
theology and philosophy flourished. During this period, the
Treatise of Hasan al-Basri (642–728 CE) argued that man
determined his own fate. Those who advocated human responsibility became known as the Qadariyya (Determiners) and
their claim was not just that each person is responsible for
his or her actions, but that governments, too, are responsible for their actions. Their theological position backed their
political critique of the ruling Umayyad dynasty, which had
assumed authority on the premise that they had been appointed
by God. The Mu'tazilites (Separatists) emerged out of the
Qadariyya and gave equal weight to reason and revelation as
sources of religious knowledge and truth. They became the

official court school in Baghdad in the 800s CE. The Mu'tazilites emphasized God's unity and justice and argued that God was just and that man alone was responsible for his good and bad actions. God has shown the right way through prophecy and revelation, but when God promised salvation for righteous action, or damnation for serious transgression, then he would deliver accordingly for he can only act according to his just nature.

This rationalist approach to Muslim theology was superseded by the Ashari school of thought in the tenth century, which reasserted the superiority of revelation over reason and predestination over free will. The concept of *kasb* (acquisition) was introduced, whereby God creates the power for a person to act at the moment of action but the person 'acquires' the consequences of his action through his own volition. Asharism also reinstated a literal reading of the anthropomorphic terms which describe God in the Qur'an with hands and eyes and sitting on the throne. They claimed that these were true statements about God except that as human beings, we don't know how God is manifested in this way. They also asserted that God was not bound by any human understanding of justice and that God as sovereign and omniscient could act in whichever way he chose. These schools of thought, part of the intellectual flourishing of Muslim societies from the eighth century onwards, are rooted in the creation story where good and evil, human free will and divine plan all come into play.

It would be fair to say that such theological concerns have long ceased to be the focus of Muslim thought and piety. Muslims have tended to consider man's purpose in life in the context of his relationship and worship of God. The mystery of existence is summed up in a haunting and beautiful hadith qudsi: 'I was a hidden treasure and I wished to be known so I created the world.'[18] Creation does not begin with man, but man's role in creation becomes central. God tells the angels that man has been formed as God's representative on earth. While the angels were right when they proclaimed that man 'would make mischief and shed blood', God defended man by revealing man's knowledge and entrusting him with a purpose. In accepting the burden as custodians of the earth, human beings undertook a sacred commitment; this commitment is no less than worship itself. By reflecting upon the beauty of nature, striving to restore the balance in nature, human beings may find a glimpse of the Divine.

6

FAITH AS RITUAL

Sura al-Muzammil (Folded in Garments) Q73:1–9,20)
O you folded in garments, stand for prayer at night but not all, half of it or a little less or a little more and recite the Qur'an in slow rhythmic tones. Soon shall we send down a heavy word. Truly the rising by night is a time when impression is more keen and speech more certain. There is for you during the day ordinary duties but keep in remembrance the name of your Lord and devote yourself to Him wholeheartedly. He is the Lord of the East and the West, there is no god but He so take Him as someone to be trusted. Your Lord knows that you stand for prayer at least two thirds of the night or half the night or a third of the night and so does a party of those with you but Allah determines night and day and knows that you are unable to keep count of it. So Allah has turned to you so that you read of the Qur'an as much as may be easy for you. He knows that there may be among you some in ill-health, others travelling through the land in pursuit of Allah's bounty and others fighting in Allah's cause. So read as much of the Qur'an as is easy for you. And establish

prayers and give zakat and loan to Allah a beautiful loan.
And whatever good you send forth for yourselves you shall
find it with Allah, indeed better and greater in reward. So
seek Allah's forgiveness for Allah is most forgiving, most
merciful.

Andrew Rippin, a contemporary scholar of Islam has
observed the role that ritual plays in defining religious
identity:

> To a person standing on the outside observing the presence
> of a religion, ritual is the most obvious sign of the charac-
> ter and existence of believers in that faith. Ritual activities
> and their attendant buildings, clothes and assorted para-
> phernalia provide the emblems of a religion and become,
> for the members of the religion themselves, modes for the
> expression of their identity.[19]

For the believer, participating in ritual activity is a 're-
enactment of a profound truth,'[20] that which makes one
belong to a belief system drawing the believer and the community of believers near to God. Yet despite its central role,
the essence of a religious belief cannot be grasped by simply
observing ritual practice. Ritual can mark, identify and sepa-
rate a community of believers, it can point to what is held
most sacred in terms of rites and worship, but it can never
quite capture faith, for faith transcends form and imagery.
This is particularly true of Islam, where faith is presented as a
gradual process from Islam (surrender) to *iman* (faith) to the
final state of *ihsan* (doing good). Belief in God is a deeper state
of awareness, of conviction and of humility, all of which ultimately lie beyond ritual.

The life of the practising Muslim can be seen as perpetual
worship where the profane and the sacred are intimately connected through ritual and ritualism. However, the Qur'an has
very few injunctions about individual or communal ritual.
The overriding message of the Qur'an is that in worship man
enters a covenant with God. In Islam rituals are a means by
which we remember God's presence in daily life; rituals keep
us connected with the transcendent.

In worship, as laid out in the Qur'an, ritual centres on five
activities. These are the *shahada*, the declaration that 'There is
no god but God and Muhammad is His Messenger'; the salat,
formal prayers performed five times a day; *zakat*, obligatory
almsgiving; *sawm*, fasting in the month of Ramadan and the
hajj, the annual pilgrimage to Mecca. Any introductory
course on Islam in a Western university will teach that these
are the central prescriptive features of Muslim life and piety.
The Qur'an particularly emphasizes prayer and almsgiving as
righteous activities, but it is a hadith which first suggested that
these five core activities were central 'pillars':

> Islam has been built on five [pillars] testifying that there is
> no god but God and that Muhammad is the Messenger of
> Allah, performing the prayers, paying the alms, making the
> pilgrimage to the House and fasting in Ramadan.

Although the word pillar is not to be found in the Arabic
original, the hadith identifies these five practices as fundamentals of the faith. Another saying suggests that these pillars
are a pathway to paradise itself:

> A man asked the Messenger of Allah, 'Do you think that if
> I perform the obligatory prayers, fast in Ramadan, treat as

lawful that which is lawful and treat as forbidden that
which is forbidden, and do nothing further, I shall enter
paradise?' He said, 'Yes.'

These pillars are performed as a way of drawing near to
God, and if the rituals are properly observed and with the
right intention, they are also a means of self-transformation.
The worship of God, *ibada*, is not confined though to obeying
ritual and observing the law. Alongside prostration in ritual
prayer, a physical reflection of humility, worship is also about
man's heightened awareness of the bond he has with his fellow
men. Obedience should not be equated with servility, rather
an enhanced awareness of what man is in God's eyes, how he
can realize his own worth and potential through exercising self-
autonomy, and the respect and dignity, *izza*, which must form
the basis of his relations with fellow beings. For the Muslim
mystics known as Sufis, external rituals are symbolic of an
inner journey towards God, the ultimate and only reality.

The first pillar, *shahadah*, means testimony and refers to a
simple creed recited during prayer and other forms of worship. All believers and converts to Islam are required to utter
these words, 'There is no god but God and Muhammad is the
Messenger of God.'

The second pillar, salat, is the performance of regular
prayers. In a meeting between God and Muhammad referred
to briefly in the Qur'an, Muhammad negotiated the number
of times a believer should pray. The Qur'an records the event
in the following verse:

Praise be to him who brought his servant by night from the
sacred mosque to the farthest mosque whose vicinity we
have blessed so that we might show him our signs. (Q17:1)[21]

This Qur'anic verse is elaborated in great detail in later
hadith literature. Whether it was a dream or a real experience,
it has historically received great literary and devotional attention by the Sufis. Muhammad travelled during the night on a
marvellous horse-like animal called Buraq from Mecca to
Jerusalem (*isra'*) and from Jerusalem ascended through the
various heavens (*mi'raj*) where he met all the prophets of the
past, until he finally came into the presence of God himself.
This ascension is Muhammad's greatest spiritual experience.
On his return to the seventh heaven, Muhammad conversed
with Moses about his meeting with God. Muhammad said he
was instructed by God to order the community to pray fifty
times per day. Moses advised Muhammad that the people
would never be able to observe fifty prayers. Muhammad
returned to God who granted a reduction. Moses suggested
he ask for a further reduction. This continued until
Muhammad finally returned with the number five. Even then,
Moses thought that the community would not manage to
observe this many prayers. Muhammad replied that he was
now too ashamed to ask God again.

This narrative demonstrates how the life and prophecy of
Muhammad is inextricably intertwined with the defining
ritual practices of Islam. Anyone who has visited a Muslim
country will be aware of the five daily calls to prayer – the
adhan. This formal prayer is a constant reminder to the
believer to remember God in normal daily life; that worshipping God is a route to individual prosperity. Before formal
prayer, one is required to perform ablutions with water; where
water is unavailable, clean dust or sand will suffice. Muslims
pray facing the direction of Mecca in a congregation in a
mosque, at home on their own or with their family. When
praying in a congregation, people stand behind an Imam,

who is entrusted to lead the prayer. Whether prayer is individual or congregational, it is the heart of Muslim worship and has become one of the defining features of Islamic societies.

The third pillar is zakat (almsgiving). Alongside prayer, almsgiving is one of Islam's principal obligations. Every adult Muslim is obliged to pay 2.5% of their wealth accumulated over a year to those in need in the Muslim community. Almsgiving should not be confused with charity, which is a voluntary act. The word 'zakat' also has connotations of virtue and purity: by contributing to the poor and needy or for the general welfare of society, one's remaining wealth is purified. The obligation of almsgiving demands that Muslims develop a social conscience in which the accumulation of wealth and the distribution of wealth are twin pillars of a strong and unified society. In some Muslim countries, government assumes responsibility for collection of zakat. In non-Muslim societies, the payment is largely a matter of individual conscience. Many Muslims nowadays, unaware of how much and where to contribute, donate to various Muslim and non-Muslim relief and charitable organizations. By doing this, the spirit of giving and its transformative potential remains alive in Muslim communities.

The fourth pillar is *sawm* (fasting). Many of my Muslim friends at school avoided formal prayer or any regular reading of the Qur'an but were always observant of fasting in Ramadan. This baffled me, partly because I found fasting difficult but also because they believed fasting the ultimate expression of Muslim piety. Fasting during the month of Ramadan is still one of the most well-known of Muslim practices. Food and drink is not taken between the hours of sunrise and sunset, and the believer must also abstain from

sexual relations during these hours. Women during menstruation, pregnancy or immediately after childbirth, are exempt
from fasting, as are travellers, the infirm and the sick.
Although most Muslim families encourage young children to
keep some of the fasts as practice before observing the full fast,
this is not a requirement. Fasting comes to an end with the
canonical Feast of Fast-Breaking at the end of the month
known as the Eid al-Fitr.

When the fast is broken at sunset, families often meet and
share the food. Ramadan can be a challenging time, particularly when it falls in the summer. The Muslim calendar is a
lunar calendar, eleven days shorter than a Gregorian calendar
and this means that dates of events in the Islamic lunar calendar move forward about eleven days every year. In recent
years, many Muslims have questioned whether the practice of
fasting can be changed during summer months when the sun
sets very late. And, as Muslims settle in the West and face the
demands of the workplace, they have questioned whether
there may be some form of concession or exemption. These
questions have met with a variety of theological responses
but there is a general reluctance to change in any serious way
the traditional parameters of Ramadan, which has always been
regarded as a core of the faith. The paradox of Ramadan is
that although fasting can be physically difficult, the actual
month is one of celebration and joy: this was when the
Qur'an was revealed. The believer often slows down daily
activities to devote more time to religious reflection and many
will go on a spiritual retreat (*itikaf*) in a local mosque spend-
ing day and night in prayer and worship.

Once in a lifetime, if health and wealth permits, an adult
Muslim will travel to Mecca to perform the fifth pillar of the
faith, the hajj. This pilgrimage is observed between the eighth

and twelfth days of Dhu al-Hijja, the last month of the Islamic lunar calendar. The hajj is a defining moment in the Muslim calendar, and several million people from all backgrounds and cultures gather at Mecca. The visual image most associated with the hajj is a sea of black and white movement around the Ka'ba, the black draped cubical structure in Mecca dedicated by Muhammad to God.[22] Although the hajj is in some ways the pinnacle of the Muslim year, many of the rites are a mixture of the re-enactment of the sacrifice Abraham was asked to make of his son, Ishmael, by God[23] and practices which date back to pre-Islamic times.

Traditionally most Muslims would go on the hajj in the later part of their lives, when they no longer have family or financial commitments, but the last decade has seen a rise in younger Muslims going on the hajj. They prioritize the pilgrimage, not wishing to defer it for any reason. There is also a trend for couples to make the pilgrimage almost immediately after marriage. The pilgrimage is being seen increasingly as a uniting force between Muslims. Pilgrims brought together in their faith and mission, converging from all corners of the world, become a powerful image of Muslim unity and identity.

The real challenge of the hajj is not the physical labours but the spiritual transformation it effects. Focusing on God demands that we reflect on ourselves, look within at what we need to change, what we must overcome and what we need to do for others. All religious occasions bring people together, unite them momentarily towards a common goal and purpose, but this kind of unity, however grand and inspiring, is momentary. The real challenge of our life is not how we rejoice in the occasional shared unity but how we go back to dealing with daily differences with those who look different, who think differently, whose faith is different. We cannot rely on mass gatherings and religious occasions, where our experience is one of shared unity, to help us. Instead, we should be prepared to face our inner prejudices as individuals.

As well as the five pillars, there are countless other forms of devotion in worship. Ritual purity, for instance, is a fundamental part of Muslim worship, the very threshold of worship. It is a formalized manner of washing for the purpose of prayer and handling the Qur'an. The Qur'an is doubly sacred, because of the divine origin of its content, and because the physical book itself is considered sacred. Islamic law divides impurities into minor and major categories, where natural bodily functions like urinating, menstruation, breaking wind and sexual intercourse determine whether minor or major ablutions are needed. Although most Muslims adhere to these rituals many argue that prayer itself is more important and should be observed with the right intention whether or not the correct purification rituals have been carried out. The right intention is fundamental to any worship and reflects integrity before God. Without the right intention, the ethical dimension of ritual is lost.

Marriage, childbirth and death are all accompanied by rituals. Male circumcision, neither mentioned in the Qur'an nor strictly required by the *shari'a*, is carried out in Muslim societies as another form of ritual purity. Not all ritual practices are either uniform or accepted in the Muslim world, but there is a tendency by outsiders to see Muslims as a single community, all assiduously adhering to the same ritual practices, despite the growing diversity of the Muslim world.

The tension between faith and works has long been an area of debate in Islam. In the early period of Islam, theologians tried to establish who could be considered a Muslim.

Could someone who had committed a grave sin continue to be called a believer? A group called the Murjiites, who received considerable support from many mainstream scholars such as the Hanafi school, argued that faith was unaffected by works. They claimed that if a person did not observe the practice of Islam or even if he committed a grave sin, he could not be called an infidel. Basing their arguments on such prophetic hadith as 'whoever says, there is no God but Allah and dies in that belief will enter paradise', the Murjiites established that faith was always distinct from works because works were external and faith came from the heart.

The debate continues today with a modern twist. While earlier scholars tried to liberate faith from the trappings of external ritual and even major sins, many Muslims today regard ritual as the definitive expression of true faith. This is not confined to prayer or fasting but extends to the practical interpretation of an Islam which existed during the time of the Prophet. The growing visibility of the *hijab* (female head covering) and now *niqab* (full face covering) is just one example of how Muslims regard faith and observance as inextricably intertwined; the more Muslim you look, the stronger your faith in God.

While ritual is a symbol of devotion, it can also be used as a way to control society. Religious identity excludes as well as binds. Although religious conviction may seem noble, our personal faith should never lull us into any complacency, nor should we arrogantly think we have all the answers. True faith is ultimately about asking questions and remaining open to a plurality of ways of understanding God. Just as the Qur'an encourages the believer to remember God in prayer and worship, previous revelations established similar ways of drawing near to God. During the hajj, Muslims re-enact the humble submission Abraham showed to God. Throughout the hajj, they are strengthened in a global *umma* or brotherhood. Perhaps the umma of the Muslims must find a way of translating itself into the fraternity of all people. Many Muslims will not agree that the umma should or could ever be about a common brotherhood of all humanity. But Muslims have a precedent in the actions of Muhammad himself. In order to bring to an end the bitter feuding between the various clans and tribes in Medina, Muhammad drafted a constitution when he arrived there in 622 CE. The Constitution of Medina ensured the security of the community and guaranteed religious freedom for the Muslims, Jews and the pagans who were now within the fold of a single community or umma. Umma has evolved to mean the universal community or brotherhood of Muslims only. This has been a largely historical construction of the word and one must question whether this definition of brotherhood can ever promote deeper levels of inclusivity in society or whether it will always be reflective of exclusive and divisive visions of society. Despite the political and social differences between Medina in the seventh century and now, the spirit of the Constitution of Medina should be revived.

7

MODESTY AND MODERNITY

Sura Nisa (The Women) Q4:1–3;34, Sura al-Nur (The Light) Q24:30–31

O people, revere your Lord who created you from a single soul, and created from it his mate and from the two scattered countless men and women. Revere God of whom you make demands and revere the wombs for God watches over you. Restore to orphans their property and do not substitute your worthless possessions for their good ones and do not devour their wealth with your wealth for that is a great sin. If you fear that you will not be able to deal justly with the orphans, marry women of your choice, two, three or four but if you fear that you will not be able to deal with them justly, then only one, or what your right hands possess; that will be more suitable to prevent you from doing injustice.

Men are the maintainers of the affairs of women as God has preferred some of them over others, and by what they spend of their wealth.

And say to the believing men that they should lower their gaze and guard their modesty that will make for greater

purity for them: And Allah is well acquainted with all that
they do. And say to the believing women that they should
lower their gaze and guard their modesty; that they should
not display their ornaments except what appears thereof;
that they should draw their veils over their bosoms and not
display their beauty except to their husbands.

Over the last few decades, gender relations has become one of
the most controversial aspects of Qur'anic discourse and
Muslim societies. Despite the concerted effort by scholars
and Muslim communities to find a consistent narrative, there
is no overall Qur'anic view of women just as there is no overall Qur'anic view of men. Only one sura addresses women
specifically and elsewhere women are alluded to in a group
such as the 'wives of the Prophet', there are named individuals such as Mary, or they are referred to in generic terms. Both
men and women are recipients of the divine moral message
and despite variations on social and legal issues such as marriage, divorce and inheritance, they will be punished or
rewarded equally for their actions:

For Muslim men and women, for believing men and
women, for devout men and women, for truthful men and
women, for men and women who are patient and constant,
for men and women who humble themselves. For men and
women who give in charity, for men and women who fast
and deny themselves, for men and women who engage
much in Allah's praise, for them Allah has prepared forgiveness and a great reward. (Q33:35)

Such spiritual egalitarianism is inherent in the Qur'an.
Nevertheless, the Qur'an poses a particular challenge for those

trying to translate this spiritual egalitarianism into social equalities. There are three popular discourses in the discussion of gender relations in the Qur'an. One argument is to say that the Qur'an gave women various rights but patriarchal systems have throughout history marginalized, even silenced women's demands for autonomy; the second acknowledges that the Qur'an may have improved women's positions from the pre-Islamic period, but that the Qur'an infantilized women; the third believes that the Qur'an saw clearly that men were the providers in society and had autonomy over the affairs of women even though men should respect the rights women were given. These three positions arise from the Qur'anic verses above but other hadith sources support varying perspectives. Muslims also look to historical figures from Muhammad's life to understand the role of women in Islamic society. Muhammad's wives Khadijah and Aisha are considered exemplary: knowledgeable, virtuous, intellectual and exercising self-autonomy. The Prophet's own household is often described as the ideal family life within a polygamous framework, and hadith such as 'The best of you is he who is the best among you to his wife', is quoted to claim that Muhammad was sympathetic and generous towards women. In addition, the Qur'anic verses which state that women cannot be inherited, have a right to own their wealth and that within marriage must be given their bridewealth and receive maintenance, all indicate a desire to give women rights and dignity. The Qur'an fundamentally promotes egalitarianism, in that early Islam favoured female participation whether it be in the mosques or in learning, but these favourable attitudes faded over time with the subordination of women in private and public life. While women were not denied access to learning and were even engaged in religious discussions, the

extent of their influence in the intellectual and public life of
the evolving Muslim communities is difficult to measure.
There seems to be consensus that although Muhammad himself was fairly sympathetic to women, some of his own
companions did not encourage female participation in the
emerging Muslim community. As Islam spread, scripture and
empire did not encourage female self-determination. Asma
Barlas writes:

> The Abbasids also did irreparable harm to women by insti-
> tutionalizing female slavery and subordination to men
> through the practice of popularizing limitless harems, the
> stuff of legends like the 'Arabian Nights'. As a result, over
> time, the tradition of historicizing women as active, full
> participants in the making of culture came to be replaced
> by a memory in which women had no right to equality.[24]

In the West, largely polarized and categorical views of
Muslim women remain. Muslim women tend to be regarded
as a monolithic, subjugated group, and the criticisms are often
made through the prism of Western feminism, anxious to
apply its own vision of success on Muslim societies. The
American feminist Phyllis Chesler, author of a recent book
The Death of Feminism, criticized contemporary feminists for
hiding behind multicultural relativism and refusing to speak
out against some of the more oppressive, even barbaric practices in Muslim countries. Practices considered normal in
some Islamic cultures, though their Islamic origin is disputed,
have attracted global attention. The most significant example
is the widespread practice of female circumcision, more commonly known as 'female genital mutilation'. A number of
African and Arab countries have retained this practice to

control female sexual drive and autonomy and preserve traditional concepts of chastity and family honour.[25]

The issue of honour is fundamental in gender relations and in the way modesty has been conceptualized in many Muslim societies. I believe strongly that modesty for both men and women is an intrinsic part of the Islamic faith but has been conceptualised in the Qur'an through an emphasis on chastity. Chastity demands that men and women do not enter into illicit sexual relations such as fornication or adultery, and flogging and stoning became the established punishment in classical law for such sins. Marriage is the only appropriate context for sexual relations for both men and women. Classical law demands that girls and boys marry soon after puberty, when they become aware of their sexual appetites. Marriage allows them to enjoy sex within a legally and socially accepted framework. The concept of young, free and single does not in arise in Muslim law. The emphasis on chaste behaviour is reinforced by largely segregated cultures, structured to prohibit the free intermingling of young people. It is this free intermingling which will lead to *fitnah* or seductive acts; when men and women intermingle freely, it is women who are regarded as primarily responsible for leading men sexually astray. If the Qur'anic world talks about men and women largely through the prism of marriage, contemporary life throws up one of the biggest challenges facing Muslims in the West – the young, unmarried person who lives and works alongside those of other faiths and cultures. The traditional Islamic legal system sees a natural progression from childhood to puberty to marriage; this no longer applies.

Unfortunately, concepts of modesty and honour have remained largely focused on female clothing and gender segregation. Modesty directly and indirectly makes women the bearers of honour and shame, the repository of sexual ethics and family values. When they keep themselves away from public gaze, it is not just their honour they are preserving, but the honour of the faith itself. Yet, equating shame and honour with particular forms of clothing does not address the more complex issues of modesty and moral behaviour. Men and women may dress differently in Muslim societies but sex outside marriage and adultery are still issues within these societies. The increased emphasis on covering alone distracts from much of the abusive and oppressive behaviour that also occurs under the guise of honour and modesty. The most common examples are women being forced into marriage and restriction on women's freedom and ability to exercise their legal rights.

That some Muslim women are choosing to wear the veil is being seen in the West as a symbol of the failure of multiculturalism. In 2006, Jack Straw, British Labour MP for Blackburn and former Foreign Secretary, created a national furore when he suggested that Muslim women should take off their face veils, which he believes are a sign of separation. The increasing visibility of the headscarf (now commonly known as the hijab) and the niqab (full face veil) has been one of the most potent signs of Muslim female identity in recent years. Muslim and non-Muslim voices argued for and against veiling, and right to self-expression. Some commentators reiterated the ever popular 'clash of civilizations' theory by Samuel Huntington in which Huntington postulates the eventual clash between a progressive Western civilization and an arcane Muslim world.[26] Should a piece of clothing attract such furore? The veil no longer conjures up images of the mystery and lure of the East, but has come to represent everything the West has struggled against. The niqab symbolizes a barrier to open communication, gender equality, and to comfortable and open relations between men and women. For many, it is a medieval concept with no place in modern life. Women who have begun to wear the full veil over the last few years, just like those who adopted the hijab before them, argue that the distinctions about modern and pre-modern life are superfluous. Veiling in some form is an essential aspect of their piety and devotion to God; for them, it may not be Qur'anic in prescription, but it is certainly Qur'anic in spirit.

During the nineteenth century Arab feminists such as Qasim Amin and Rifaat Tahtawi argued that veiling and female seclusion were signs of the social backwardness of Islamic societies. Unless women were educated in a formal sense, Muslim societies would not prosper. Today, more and more Muslim women who are both educated and working outside the home are demanding the right to wear the veil, partly because Islam has been politicized and partly because many want to assert their Muslim identity in a wider non-Muslim society. This trend has created problems in Europe. France's laicite laws have prohibited the hijab in schools as part of the ban on all religious symbols in public schools. A number of cities in Germany have prohibited women from wearing the hijab in public institutions. And within Muslim communities, veiling remains at the forefront of social, theological and political debate. For many it is considered a litmus test for individual piety, but for others, like the Moroccan sociologist Fatima Mernissi, veiling and segregation are not grounded in the Qur'an. Mernissi argues that women and minorities are the final test for the Muslim states, which must modernize their laws, to conform with the principle of equality that the Qur'an teaches is a fundamental value.[27]

Even if it is conceded that patriarchal social structures have strongly suppressed Qur'anic egalitarianism, denying women any real voice, it is easy to see how the above verses which open the chapter may have encouraged men to keep women subordinate. The specific historical circumstances of the Qur'anic revelation give a better understanding. Permission to take more than one wife, albeit with conditions, was granted after the Battle of Uhud when the Muslim community was left with many orphans and widows who needed protection. Early Muslim exegetes and some contemporary scholars acknowledge these historical circumstances as a way of explaining the social relevance of polygamy. They argue that the Qur'an did not introduce but rather restricted polygamy, which was unrestricted during the jahiliyya period. Polygamy was a solution to a particular situation and not an eternal male prerogative. However, in recent years, the verses, 'But if you fear that you will not be able to deal with them justly, then only one', have received greater attention by Muslims, legislators and scholars, all of whom argue that there is an inherent moral and social imbalance in the way polygamy has developed as a social institution. They claim that the Qur'an's reference to acting justly to wives is actually a direct exhortation to monogamy. When the Muslim country of Tunisia made polygamy illegal, it reflected society's willingness to accept change and develop a new interpretation of the Qur'an.

The Qur'anic world saw men as the providers in society, describing them as *qawwamun* (maintainers). The word contains the sense of having ascendancy or superiority. Some classical exegetes and contemporary scholars have insisted that as providers, men have a degree of authority over women. Yet in our contemporary world many have argued that women who work outside the home are no longer being 'maintained' and that it was only the economic distinction of that period which allowed men to be guardians over women; today men and women provide and protect for each other. Their view is backed by another verse in the Qur'an, 'From God's signs is that God created mates for you among yourselves so that you may find repose and tranquillity with them, and God has created love and compassion between you (Q30:21).

In recent years, many scholars have argued that despite verses which reflect a male privilege in the Qur'an, it was not the Qur'an but the hadith attributed to Muhammad which promoted female subservience:

> It is not lawful for anyone to prostrate to anyone else. But if I would have ordered anyone to prostrate to another, I would have commanded wives to prostrate to their husbands because of the enormity of the rights of husbands over their wives.[28]

> If a man calls his woman to bed and she refuses to come, the angels will continue to curse her until the morning.[29]

Such hadith pose serious questions about how and when Muhammad responded to theological questions, and they conflict with many of the stories of conjugal love between Muhammad and his own wives. Significantly, they go against the Qur'an's essential message which calls for mutual love and understanding in marriage, where husband and wife should be like 'garments for each other' (Q2:187). If such hadith have contributed to women's denigration, Muslim societies must face up to the moral, theological and social consequences of such words. Muslims must have the courage to accept that hadith which jar with concepts of divine mercy, human dignity or contemporary notions of human rights, should be read in light of their particular contexts. If they are in conflict with the broader, ethical principles of the Qur'an, these hadith should not be allowed to continue as part of normative Islam. Human beings have been created free and moral agents who must use individual and collective reason to improve the moral framework of society for all.

The diverse lifestyle that Muslims everywhere are leading now is witness to the fact that difficult choices are being made and decisions being taken within and outside of public discourse. Women in Muslim societies are divorcing, having abortions and having sexual relations outside marriage. Their freedom must therefore form part of mainstream discourse. In this discourse men and women must work together with integrity to create a more harmonious and respectful society. They both require courage and the support of their 'mate'.

This view is still too revolutionary for many. It demands that women's rights to make choices are recognized and considered valuable. Muslim women are proud of their faith; for many women, the real struggle is how they reconcile their faith, their cultural tradition and their immediate familial contexts with the overarching impetus of feminism – the right to autonomy. Female autonomy is not un-Islamic but it can mean at times taking risks, going against community expectations and reaching out for male support; for some it can be the biggest struggle of their lives.

8

JEWS AND CHRISTIANS – BELIEVERS OR DENIERS?

Sura al-Baqarah (The Cow) Q2:62
Those who believe and those who have been Jews and the
Christians and the Sabians, whoever believes in God and
the last day and does good, their reward awaits them with
their Lord and no fear shall be on them and neither will
they have sorrow.

Sura al-Kafirun (The Ones Who Deny) Q109
Say: O you who deny, I worship not what you worship nor
will you worship what I worship. And I will not worship
what you worship nor will you worship that which I worship;
To you your way and to me mine.

The Qur'an says that Muslims must be open to the existence
of other faiths. The suras which refer to people of other faiths
have come into sharper focus in recent years with the spread
of inter-religious discourse and the emphasis on pluralism.
The Qur'an accepts religious diversity while warning against
the errors of other religious communities. Muslims therefore
have a double task; how to understand pluralism as referenced

in the Qur'an and how Islam fits into our contemporary plu-
ralistic world. The Qur'an mentions Jews and Christians
several times, yet these groups would not recognize themselves
as described in the Qur'an. Moses and the Jewish tribes are
mentioned repeatedly but as a nation which ignored God's
commands and blessings. Jesus and Christianity are referred to
but often to refute the Trinity. Nevertheless, the above verses
are well-used in inter-religious discussions to demonstrate
Islam's inherent openness to previous prophets and their mes-
sages, especially the Jews and Christians. God's message – that
there is one true God – was revealed to prophets prior to
Muhammad. They preached against worshipping multiple
gods and warned people about the Hereafter. The message
given to the Arabs in the seventh century is the same message
given to the Jews and Christians earlier. The Qur'an then
confirms previous books, revelations and prophets, but it still
sees itself as distinct from these earlier revelations. It thus
paints a varied picture of those other faiths and its attitude
towards Jews and Christians remains ambivalent.

The central Qur'anic message calls for belief in the one
God and those who do not share this message are charged
with varying levels of unbelief, ingratitude and denial, all contained in the word kufr. False belief is the focus of much
theological discussion. How should the Muslim relate in words
and action towards people who do not accept the monotheism
of the Qur'an? Although the distinction is not always clear, the
Qur'an appears to distinguish between two lots of 'other'; the
mushrik or polytheists, and the *ahl al-kitab* or People of the
Book, as Jews, Judaism, Christians and Christianity are commonly known. They are mentioned some fifty-four times in
the Qur'an. In some suras, the Qur'an includes their followers
as believers; in others it is the believers themselves who have

corrupted their original scriptures and have fallen outside the true path. Judaism and Christianity are often grouped together in the Qur'an although the Qur'anic view of them differs on points of dogma or moral character.

The words used for Christians in the Qur'an is *nasara*, derived from Jesus's home town of Nazareth in Galilee. When the Qur'an picks out Christian themes, it particularly focuses on the conventional Christian doctrine, where Jesus is 'son of God' and part of the Trinity:

> Certainly they disbelieve who say, 'Allah is Christ the son of Mary.' But said Christ, 'O children of Israel, worship Allah, my Lord and your Lord, whoever joins other gods with Allah, Allah will forbid him the gardens and the fire will be his abode . . .' they disbelieve those who say Allah is one of three for there is no god except one God. (Q5:72–3)

> 'O people of the Book, commit no excesses in your religion nor say of Allah except the truth. Christ Jesus the son of Mary was the Messenger of Allah and His word, which he bestowed on Mary and a spirit proceeding from him. So believe in Allah and his messengers. Do not say three; desist, it will be better for you for Allah is One and glory be to Him. (Q4:141)

Scholars have argued that in its direct references to Christian beliefs and practices as well as its judgements of them, the Qur'an is referring to Syrian ascetics and preachers; the Qur'an views the piety of the monks and their practices in a favourable light:

> You will find the people most hostile to the believers are the Jews and the idolaters. You will surely find those closest in

friendship to the believers to be those who say 'We are
Christians.' That is because among them are priests and
monks and because they are not arrogant. (Q5:82–3)

Though the piety of the Christians is apparently praised in
this verse, the Qur'an does not endorse Christian monasticism
and later says, 'But the monasticism they invented for themselves, we did not prescribe for them' (Q57:27). And although
Christian friendship is mentioned here, Muslims are urged to
remain guarded against the Christians for they are not true
friends of Islam, 'O you who believe, take not the Jews and
Christians for your protectors; they are but the friends and
protectors to each other' (Q5:51).

The Qur'anic verses referring to Christians and Jews were
revealed when Muhammad resided in Medina from 622
onwards. Muhammad was invited to Medina by Jewish tribes
who hoped he would unite them in their own tribal conflicts.
Muhammad had accepted in 622 CE, partly to flee persecution
in Mecca, and he was assisted by those who emigrated with
him, the *muhajirun*, who wished to help him establish the new
Muslim community in Medina. Some Jews within the host
community converted to Islam and became known as the
helpers (*ansar*). In time the relationship between Muhammad,
the Jews, the muhajirun and the ansar was formally outlined in
a document known as the Constitution of Medina, a document
which underlines how serious Muhammad was in uniting all
believers into a single community or umma. Martin Lings, the
Sufi scholar, writes that this document 'formed all of them
into a single community of believers but allowing for differences
between the two religions'.[30] The number of verses promising
divine reward to 'those who believe and who do good work'
can be interpreted as a reward to anyone who has submitted to

God, which includes Jews and Christians. Jews and Christians are united with the Muslims through the common bonds of their belief in God, belief in prophets and divine books.[31] They are unlike the idolaters (mushrikun) and unbelievers (kafirun), who share no heritage of true belief with the Muslims. Jews and Christians are among those for whom 'their wages await them with their lord and no fear shall there be on them and neither shall they sorrow'(Q2:62). Muslims should relate to the People of the Book only in the best way (Q29:46). They were given protected status under Muslim dominion; they could not be forced into conversion as God would distinguish among them in the Hereafter (Q22:18).

Despite the Qur'an's acceptance of Christians and Jews, it is only partial. The Qur'an warns the Jews that they have strayed from the path. One of the longest verses in the Qur'an alludes to God's acts of mercy for his chosen people:

O children of Israel, call to mind the blessings which I bestowed upon you and that I preferred you to all others. Then guard yourselves age a day when one soul shall not avail another nor shall intercession be accepted for her . . . and remember we delivered you from the people of Pharaoh; they set you hard tasks and chastisement, slaughtered your sons and let your womenfolk live . . . and remember we divided the sea for you and saved you, drowned Pharaoh's people within your very sight. And remember We appointed forty nights for Moses and in his absence you took the calf and you did extremely wrong. Even then We did forgive you so that you would be grateful. And remember we gave Moses the Book and the criterion (between right and wrong) so you would be rightly guided. (Q2: 47–53)

Such verses reveal the frustration God felt with the Jewish people, the 'chosen people' at one point in history but who gradually rejected or forgot God's blessings. Despite establishing a certain harmony between the fledgling Muslim community and the Jewish people of Medina, over time a subtle change in attitude to the Jews is reflected in the Qur'anic verses. Many of the verses paint Jews as an arrogant community who believed they were chosen by God, who repeatedly rejected God's favours and signs, who had appropriated the figure of Abraham for themselves and who ultimately refused to heed Muhammad's new message. They are even associated with hypocrites: those who 'believe with their lips but whose hearts have no faith'(Q5:41). Muhammad's gradual dissention with the Jews on theological as well as political grounds led to some of the changes in established Muslim ritual practices. Formal prayers were originally performed in the direction of Jerusalem and then moved to Mecca. Fasting had originally followed Jewish days and practices but was now fixed in the month of Ramadan.

The Qur'an also contains verses openly critical of both the Jews and the Christians for not accepting Muhammad's prophecy or recognizing the true nature of monotheism. This has led some scholars to question which communities the Qur'an alludes to when it mentions People of the Book. M. Sharon states:

> Except for a few cases, ahl al-kitab in the Qur'an does not necessarily refer to either Jews or Christians . . . Based on the Qur'anic text, it is impossible to be more specific about the identity of ahl al-kitab with whom the Prophet had ideological, doctrinal and physical confrontations. Part of them he succeeded in making believers while against others he had to fight to the end . . . Whether defined as

Jews or Christians, ahl al-kitab were by the end of the prophet's lifetime, accused of having forsaken the true monotheistic religion of old prescribed in their books and of having adopted polytheistic doctrines that put them in the same camp as the idolators.[32]

The Qur'an does not deny salvation to Jews and Christians who do good work, by virtue of their monotheism, but it invites people of those communities to a shared religious commitment and loyalty with the new community of believers:

> People of the book come now to a word common between us and you, that we serve none but God, and that we associate nothing with him, bear witness that we are Muslims. (Q3:64).

Throughout the Qur'an the tension remains between Islam as the only path to salvation and the salvific status of Jewish and Christian monotheism. Even classical exegetes like Muhammad b. Jarir al-Tabari (d.923), who argued for the exclusive salvific status of Islam, could not see the justice in arguing for the abrogation of divine reward when the Qur'an makes no definitive claim for Islamic supersession.[33]

In contemporary debates, pluralists argue that God himself desires diversity although why God wills human diversity remains a mystery. They support their stance by quoting Qur'anic verses such as:

> To every one of you we have appointed a Law and a way. If God had so willed he would have made you a single community. But God's purpose is to test you in what he has given each of you, so strive in the pursuit of virtue. (Q5:49)

In the Qur'an, diversity essentially documents differences of belief – the non-believer is one with whom God will deal with in the Hereafter but with whom the Muslim in this life must still coexist and engage socially and politically. History bears witness to the relative tolerance and pluralism of many of the great Muslim civilizations. Perhaps this tolerance and respect owes much to the political dominance and cultural superiority of Islamic civilizations, when the Muslim world considered itself impregnable to weakness or demise. The contemporary situation is very different. Today Muslim civilizations are in the shadow of the West and a determined effort is needed to restore the principles of coexistence, to establish an intercommunal ethics that accepts a form of pluralism based on equality for all.

The problem of religious pluralism is not that the Qur'an may or may not lack a systematic theology regarding the relationship between believers, non-Muslim believers, non-believers and every other category of person. The essential question is how do Muslims see their engagement in society with people of other faiths or no faiths? A minority religion in the West, Islam has recently come under criticism as a faith which nurtures intolerant theological orientations, and which clashes with the fundamental values of democracies such as pluralism and human rights. These accusations have been exacerbated since the 9/11 attacks and the subsequent 'war on terror' sees militant extremism now firmly associated with the faith. Notwithstanding the international politics which have led to the rise in terrorist activities, there is the sense that Muslims have failed the multiculturalism experiment and not integrated into Western societies or supported liberal values. While this is debatable, there is no doubt that there has been a gradual rise in the 'us' and 'them' mentality among many

Muslims who feel that both Islam and the Muslim world are under siege and that Western liberalism is little more than moral relativism.

Such sentiments are increasingly prevalent. A rhetoric of Islam against the West has taken on many forms. Although contested by many Muslims, this rhetoric permeates much of religious and public discourse. In recent times, it has been subsumed in the West under the label of jihad, a term which has become synonymous with 'holy war'. Although the word does not translate as 'holy war', a European invention, it remains largely associated with aggression and struggle for a religious cause. The original meaning of jihad is 'striving' or 'exertion in the path of God'. In some Muslim circles jihad is regarded as a sixth pillar of Islam because it denotes an inner struggle. The spiritual struggle of the individual over his own weaknesses and sins invokes a broad range of ethical directives for the transformation of the individual and society and has nothing to do with war or warring of any kind. Mostly, the Qur'an places emphasis on peace and avoidance of any transgression, 'If your enemy inclines towards peace, then you also incline towards peace and trust in God' (Q8:61). However, the Qur'an also contains verses which urge the believer to kill the enemies of Islam in self-defence. These two different positions can be seen as reflective of *naskh* or abrogation in the Qur'an. Scholars were divided over the precise meaning of abrogation but the Qur'an refers to this concept, 'We do not abrogate a verse or cause it to be forgotten without bringing a better one like it' (Q2:106). One understanding of abrogation was that as the Qur'an was revealed over a period of twenty-three years, God sent different commands appropriate to changing circumstances. God could cancel certain rulings by new revelation. In Mecca, where the Muslims were numerically weak, they were ordered to be patient in the face of hostility from the local communities. In Medina, the situation had changed; Muslims were now stronger and could retaliate against physical opposition. These verses should be read in their historical and political contexts but are often used to justify positions of enmity and conflict by those resentful of or politically resistant to the West. The hadith literature has added to the nobility and honour of fighting for Islam and tradition suggests that martyrdom in battle is the ultimate path to heaven. 'Angels shade martyred warriors with their wings and all who die in battle automatically enter paradise.' It is easy to see how such a complex discourse, which was bound by its own rules of clemency and mercy as well as hostility towards the unbelievers, can be used by those who wish to dominate the non-Muslim world. Jihad and all its derivatives become associated with a divinely ordained mental and physical state of war.

With the rise of religious fundamentalism, pluralism has become a huge challenge for monotheistic traditions. Religion has returned in all its power and in our globalized age even local conflicts can have global consequences. Defensive posturing will not help the Muslim world. Muslims are part of the West and must accept that the post-colonialist era in which Muslim hegemony has disappeared is the reality of the present global order. They must look within their own communities and theological resources for solutions to some of our most pressing concerns. This necessitates intra-religious as well as inter-religious dialogue. What is imperative is a level of spiritual maturity – to put aside our personal convictions or any desire for triumphalism. If the Qur'an allows for multiple understanding of Jews and Christians, Muslims as moral agents have a choice to make. Either the 'other' is an enemy of Islam or a partner and friend in the worship of one God. If God is mine, he is also yours, for he transcends any particular understanding we impose on him as individuals. This may be difficult for many who are convinced they possess the only truth. Yet if we ignore the more generous interpretation of the Qur'an, we remain constrained by our own faith and not enlarged by the faiths of others.

9

LAW AND AUTHORITY

Sura al-Baqarah (The Cow) Q2:168–72/73
O People, eat of what is on earth, lawful and good; and do
not follow the footsteps of Satan for he is to you an enemy.
For he commands you what is evil and shameful, and that
you should say of Allah that of which you have no knowledge . . . o you who believe eat of the good things that we
have provided for you. And be grateful to Allah if it is Him
you worship. He has forbidden you dead meat, and blood,
and the flesh of swine, and that on which any other name
has been invoked besides that of Allah. But if one is forced
by necessity without wilful disobedience, nor transgressing
due limits, then is he guiltless. For Allah is most merciful
and most forgiving.

To the outsider, Islam is very often perceived as a religion
which tells the faithful what is and what is not permissible in
all areas of life. The Qur'an itself states that it is a message of
eternal guidance and that 'no single thing have we neglected
in the Book' (Q6:38). The issue of correct behaviour in their
everyday lives is central for Muslims; in other words, actions

must reflect an obedience to God's will. Many western commentators have concluded that unlike Christianity, which is concerned with right belief or right doctrine, Islam focuses mainly on right action – orthopraxy. While many Muslims see in right practice a reflection of their piety, such a distinct definition does not embody the essential message of the Qur'an. Muslim theologians from the very beginning defined right belief either in response to polemical debates with non-Muslims or through the scholarly discussion of creedal formula. God's unicity was always central and belief in the afterlife, the angels and other revealed books was drawn from the Qur'an itself:

> The messenger believes in what has been revealed to him from his Lord and so do the men of faith. Each one of them believes in Allah, his angels, his books and his Messengers. We make no distinction between one and another of his messengers [they say]. (Q2:285)

Right belief is the path to salvation but it is embedded in a deeper spiritual concept: that man has a covenant with God. At the dawn of creation, God asks humanity, 'Am I not your Lord?' to which humanity answers, 'Yes, we testify' (Q7:172). By acknowledging God's sovereignty and oneness, man entered a primordial pledge with God to profess monotheism and God helped man in this pledge by sending revelation and prophets to lay the foundation for ethical behaviour. Gratitude to God is reflected then in obedience to God.

Thus, despite theological engagement with correct belief, it was the vast corpus of writings on correct behaviour which dominated the Muslim intellectual output and forms the basis for popular discourse among Muslims in contemporary times. The technical Muslim word for practical faith as ordained by God is shari'a, commonly translated into English as Islamic law.[34] This translation poses a problem for scholars of Islamic jurisprudence when conveying the sense of shari'a in English. Law implies a set of rules, a set of precepts imposed upon society, but shari'a is not a superimposed structure on society – it designates religion in its totality not just the duties which man must perform in obedience to God. Shari'a is the divine legislation of God, which man must try to understand and implement and it comprises both law and ethical behaviour. Shari'a is an ideal: God's law which the science of jurisprudence must endeavour to uncover for the spiritual and practical benefit of the faithful. This science of jurisprudence was known as *fiqh*, literally 'understanding', and around the eighth and ninth centuries, the jurists or *fuqaha* used their own technical methods of argumentation and principles of law to understand the divine will in all matters. For the jurist, the written law was a reflection of his faith, a vehicle for conveying moral and material standards within the framework of the Islamic faith. It always remained a fluid expression of the divine will. The Qur'an contains the essence of Islamic law and the vast number of hadith comment on social issues, but these two sacred authorities could not cover all areas of life and often provided little or no clarity on the complexities raised by their own injunctions. Kevin Reinhart, a contemporary American scholar of Islamic law says:

> The legists' approach makes true literalism impossible. No text is read in isolation as an isolated dictum laying down the law. Instead it is recognized that meaning does not inhere in expressions in a simple one-to-one way, but what

is meant by a text may lie entirely outside the terms of its
locutionary thrust. This realization makes true literalism
impossible or at least un-Islamic.[35]

In Sunni Islam, the predominant Muslim sect, the consensus of scholars and the use of analogical reasoning compliment
the Qur'an and the hadith; these are the four fundamental
sources of Islamic law. By the tenth century, four particular
schools, Maliki, Shafi'i, Hanafi and Hanbali, named after their
respective founders, consolidated their positions as the foremost legal schools of thought. In shi'ism, greater trust is
placed in the shi'i Imams, the divinely guided leaders, and the
independent reasoning of the jurists.

Classical legal texts cover a whole range of topics from acts of
worship such as purity and prayer, through to social matters
such as rules of marriage, inheritance, buying and selling, crimes,
slaughter of foods, oaths and warfare. They look to past authorities on each issue and very seldom is anything concluded
definitively. The style is 'open-ended'; the arguments are presented though a mix of statements, questions and hypotheses. All
human acts are divided into five legal categories – obligatory,
recommended, neutral/permissible, disapproved and forbidden.
There is a sharp distinction between words 'forbidden' – *haram*
and 'permitted' – *halal*. The two terms appear in the Qur'an as
laying the foundations of right behaviour but they are legal concepts; the primary notion is that of obedience to God. Law and
morality are part of the one whole for Muslims. When Muslims
commit an act which is forbidden, they have gone against God's
express wish and violated his law. Although both terms are used
to define broader ethical behaviour, they occur frequently when
defining food laws. The word haram also means 'sacred' but not
to define things as holy, rather things which are 'set apart'.

Out of the 6,346 verses in the Qur'an only about 500 prescribe and prohibit. The Qur'an forbids actions sparingly.
Even in the verse which opens this chapter, what appear as
clear prescriptions were appropriated by the classical jurists
into more complex discussions. The requirement that God's
name be pronounced when meat is slaughtered raises the
question of intention. How do we know that the Jews and the
Christians, whose food is lawful to Muslims (Q5:5), pro-
nounce God's name and if so with what intention? If belief in
God is at the centre of this injunction, then it does not matter
in what manner Jews and Christians slaughter for they too are
monotheists; what matters is that the name of a deity other
than God is not pronounced. The jurists formulated logical
arguments from the primary sources to guide believers on
practical issues. Their wisdom and reasoning demonstrated
the expansive nature of Islamic law.

Out of the verses which prohibit acts, only a few are well-
known in the West. Gambling, usury and intoxicants are
forbidden with varying levels of interdiction. Although these
prohibitions are generally observed in most Muslim countries,
each society takes a different approach to what is permitted and
prohibited. The covering of the head has become a central issue
in recent years, especially amongst Muslims in the West, who
increasingly believe that this covering is an obligation stated in
the Qur'an. The tensions around such debates must not be
underestimated. For some believers, the adherence to Islamic
law even in the most minute details lie at the very essence of
their faith and piety. What may seem like hair-splitting dogma is
for the faithful the modesty required of them. Conversely there
are many who argue that the principles of modesty, humility and
respect have been reduced to a simple dress code in Islam; image
has become everything.

Penal law is perhaps the most notorious feature of Islamic law in the West. Punishments for unlawful intercourse, apostasy or theft in some Muslim states often make international news and provoke global condemnation. Stemming from the hadith and the Qur'an, certain crimes were traditionally considered crimes against God and carried prescribed punishments. Stoning for adultery in Saudi Arabia and Nigeria is a stark contrast to Western law where adultery may be considered immoral but is not criminal. Such punishments are barbaric, and the interpretation of the law shows no respect for individual conscience and individual dignity. Shari'a can become a political tool, deprived of detail and complexity, the very factors which give this law its innate qualities. In classical jurisprudence, stringent evidence was required to prove crimes and the law was more flexible taking into account a wide range of circumstances. When these measures are ignored, shari'a becomes codified law. In contemporary discussions many Muslims are unaware of the complexity of shari'a as both an epistemology and a legal process. They want shari'a to give simple answers to complex questions. Islam in the West is undergoing a kind of reductionist movement in which the complexities and subtleties of human experience are ignored and morality is fixed in a literal and uncritical interpretation of texts. Islam has been imprisoned by this approach to its texts. Although ethical issues are globally debated amongst Muslims, there is an atmosphere of fear and growing intolerance within many communities; Muslims are pitted against Muslims. For many in the West, Islam has become a tool in their quest to assert a social and political identity.

The challenge of modernity lies in keeping alive a meaningful interface between the divine and the secular. But whereas the Christian world largely embraced the challenge of modernity in the Enlightenment, the Muslim world associates modernity with Western colonialism. Modernity subjugated Islam, reducing its political and religious force. Many of the social and ideological tensions of today have arisen from the vestiges of the post-colonial period. One of the most contentious is that in a world of competing moralities, where does religious authority lie? The rise of certain types of Islamism such as the Taliban in Afghanistan and the Iranian revolution have created a false impression that religion and the state are inseparable in the Muslim world. In reality, most Muslim societies are divided over who is qualified to speak authoritatively. Sunni Islam has never developed a formal clergy or religious hierarchy as a social or political force. Religious scholars did not govern nor do they govern or rule today. The precise nature of the relationship between correct rule and divine will remains elusive in the Qur'an. The Qur'anic exhortation 'let there arise out of you a band of people inviting to all that is good and enjoining what is right and forbidding what is wrong' (Q3:104) is a general directive to all people and does not point to any form of institution or governance to realize this command. The Qur'an speaks of submission to God and a life of faith but it does not touch on the relative merits of theocracy, democracy or monarchy. While justice in human relations is pivotal, any discussion of political order is absent from the Qur'an; God is the supreme arbiter.

Sunni Muslim communities in the West face a challenge: who speaks for Islam? The imam of a mosque, the community worker, the politician, the thinker and the academic all represent the religion. That these various voices have been heard in public is testament to the existence of different practices of

Islam. Yet, the lack of a clear hierarchy can also have deeply negative implications for Muslims. Those who project the narrowest views are heard globally. The Saudi cleric Ibn Baz (1912–99) argued that all non-Muslims are unbelievers, destined for divine punishment. Another example closer to home is that of Omar Bakri. Omar Bakri Muhammad (*b.*1958) lived in the UK for twenty years but was refused re-entry into Britain after a trip to the Lebanon in 2005. He led the Islamist group al-Muhajiroun until it was disbanded in 2004 and has been accused of supporting various jihadist organizations including al-Qaeda. Amongst many of his anti-Western quotes is, 'We don't make a distinction between civilians and non-civilians, innocents and non-innocents. Only between Muslims and unbelievers. And the life of an unbeliever has no value. It has no sanctity.'[36] While most Muslims dissociate themselves from such hostile attitudes to the West, an increasing number of Islamist groups who reflect attitudes widely held among Muslims also argue that shari'a law should be implemented in all circumstances. They claim that to question the applicability of shari'a is to relativize the Qur'an itself. Those who contest such attitudes are often charged with 'selling out to the West'. At a time when much of the Western world sees Islam through the prism of 'terror', a religion hijacked by al-Qaeda, Muslims are being pushed into self-reflection; it is imperative that Muslims speak out with vision and courage. Reactionary voices must be sidelined and Muslim communities with different perspectives must work together for a more inclusive future.

In the West, there is a growing awareness of the internal diversity and divisions within Islam. The primary split is between Sunni and Shi'a Muslims, which originated during the time of the Prophet. The Shi'a, or 'party' of Ali, claim that Ali should have been the rightful successor to Muhammad when Muhammad died. Ali's legitimacy to rule lay in the fact that he was the cousin and son-in-law of the Prophet. They claim that there are various hadith which designate Ali a special relationship to Muhammad and that Ali should therefore have been the first and not the fourth in line to rule when Muhammad died. The Shi'a reject the authority of the first three caliphs and have a distinct body of hadith material, much of it going back to or through the early leaders of the Shi'a community. Some of this material is different to the Sunni hadith collections. The most prominent difference between Sunni and Shi'a is in the figure of the Imam. In Sunni Islam, the Imam is one who leads a congregation into formal prayer. In Shi'ism, the Imam has spiritual authority to guide the believer. God's justice requires that the world can never be left without guidance and the Imams are proof that God sends guidance for the believers. The Imams have been designated their position from the beginning of creation and are sinless. Shi'a political theory sees leadership as a divine right for the descendants of the Prophet through Ali and his wife Fatimah, Hasan and Husein, Muhammad's grandsons and the succeeding Imams. The majority of Shi'a believe that there were twelve Imams and that the twelfth Imam has gone into hiding. However, the twelfth Imam continues to inspire earthly Shi'a leaders and will return as a messianic figure shortly before the Day of Judgement.

Wahhabism emerged in Saudi Arabia in the eighteenth century. Wahhabism combines literalist reading of scripture with the cultural practices of Saudi Arabia. It asserts itself as the pure expression of Islam and dismisses the intellectual heritage of Islamic civilization. Its teachings are hostile to non-Muslims and Wahhabis have had a history of killing other

Muslims whom they considered heretics including Sunnis, Shi'i and Sufis.

In the UK, the majority of Muslims have migrated from India and Pakistan and established Barelvi and Deobandi strands of Sunni Islam. The Barelvis regard saints as intermediaries to God, emphasize mystical practices and consider Muhammad a perfect man made of light. The Deobandis reject these beliefs. They established seminaries in India during the nineteenth century in response to British colonial rule. The study of hadith lies at the core of their curriculum and their ethical stance is to follow Muhammad as closely as possible. For the Deobandis, the Muslim's first loyalty must be to Islam and not to individual nations. Their vision of Islam is more puritanical, their attitudes towards women and non-Muslims more austere. Although they encourage the education of women, especially religious education, they promote the seclusion of women. Many of the Taliban leaders attended Deobandi-influenced seminaries in Pakistan.

Classically, Islam called for self-reflection and self-critique. Today the views of communities are homogenizing. This is not helped by the growing popularity of Muslim satellite television channels, in which opinions are sought from acclaimed 'scholars' on everything from dietary laws to relations with non-Muslims. Views become entrenched particularly over controversial issues such as intermarriage. Classical Islamic law prohibited Muslim women from marrying non-Muslim men. It is almost a taboo discussion today. Yet, as the number of Muslim women marrying outside the faith slowly and inevitably rises, Muslim society will need to address this issue. Some cannot conceive of this kind of dilution of Islam; it is easier to think of such women as non-Muslim. Yet this was a temporary prohibition in the early years of Islamic expansion to ensure that Islam continued through the paternal line. That marrying outside the faith today makes a woman an unbeliever goes against all notions of human freedom and moral agency.

Communities need to discuss whether and how religious space can be extended to incorporate women. After centuries of being silenced or marginalized, can women become challenging and authoritative voices in the mosque and within the religious leadership? The mosque is a venue for humble worship, disparate and transformative voices and not a playground for community power politics.

We cannot ignore the political, legal, intellectual and social changes of the contemporary, modern world and the challenges these pose for Islam. New situations pose new questions. Our priority must be to pluralism and justice in the complex morality of today's world. An intellectual dynamism based on justice and our own moral intellect must be able to breathe new life into discourses around Shari'a. Simply referring back to select examples from the Prophet's era will not help us to 'enjoin what is good' (Q3:104). Muslims must be courageous and active participants if they wish to keep Islam a pertinent and creative basis for society and politics. Islam is part of a global humanity and Muslims are accountable to the rest of the world for what they do in the name of Islam. Morality should be based on human rights for all, egalitarianism and a far-reaching and all-embracing mercy. Real change will take place when people accept that law and authority are not immutable. Real change will become easier when God's justice and mercy is the anchor of our thinking.

10

EMBRACING CRITICAL SCHOLARSHIP

Sura Luqman Q31:26–7
To Allah belong all the heavens and the earth. Indeed Allah
is free of all wants, worthy of all praise. And if all the trees
on the earth were pens and the oceans were ink with seven
oceans behind it to add to it, yet the words of Allah would
not be exhausted, for Allah is exalted in power and full of
wisdom.

In November 2006, the American Academy of Religion held
its annual conference in Washington DC. A special panel
discussed the *Encyclopaedia of the Qur'an*, an impressive five-
volume work on the Qur'an which had recently been
completed. The panellists were made up of some of the leading Qur'an scholars in the West and associate editors of the
EQ. One of the editors commented that in compiling the
EQ, there had been no entry under 'author'. The editor was
alluding to the constraint faced by the secular academy in
their scholarship on the Qur'an, when challenging the origin
and content of the text. Scholarly Qur'anic studies can be
divided, albeit crudely, between those who study the Qur'an

as scripture and those who study the Qur'an as text. Whereas the former focus on the content and message of the Qur'an as it has been interpreted for over 1400 years, the latter is concerned with how the Qur'an came into being, using historical-critical tools to discover 'what really happened'. Their deconstruction of the text questions its historical origins including divine authorship.

Modern Western scholarship aims to have a scientific and non-confessional approach to the study of religion. Theodor Nöldeke's *Geschichte des Qorans* (History of the Qur'an), published in German in 1860, set the tone for much of European and American scholarship on the Qur'an. Nöldeke applied the critical tools of historical study to analyse how the text came into its existing state. Nöldeke's chronology divided the suras into Meccan and Medinan and also into early, middle and late periods. Critical Western scholarship challenges Muslim beliefs and assumptions about Muhammad's prophecy, the divine origin of revelation and indeed the canonization of the text itself. More recently, the works of John Wansbrough have questioned the Muslim dating of the Qur'anic canon. Wansbrough hypothesizes that the Qur'an was compiled from various sources, heavily influenced by its Christian and Jewish milieu and that it was standardized some 200 years later than the traditional Muslim accounts. Wansbrough's work tries to sever the link between the Qur'an and Muhammad. His theory has been backed by several scholars, who cite as proof the lack of clearly dated Arabic manuscripts of the Qur'an prior to 700 CE, the variant readings of the Qur'an and the structure and style of the Qur'an itself as well as Muslim exegesis. While challenging to the orthodox Muslim communities and contested by many in the academy, such theories encourage new hermeneutical approaches to the history and meanings of the Qur'an. Muhammad Arkoun, an Algerian academic who lives in Paris, contests the basic assumptions about how the Qur'an was and is received by the reader. He criticizes both the devotional and the secular approach to the Qur'an. The secular approach fails to appreciate that a scriptural text is more than a piece of writing; it contains deep meaning for the faithful. The devotional approach is unable to systemize a methodological framework which allows for a 'scientific' approach to scripture. He wrote in a recent article in the *Encyclopaedia of the Qur'an*:

> With the exception of a handful of scholars who have had no lasting influence, all Qur'anic scholars have little regard for any methodological debate and reject, if they are not actually unaware of, questions of an epistemological nature. They are sensitive only to discussing the facts according to the meaning and in the cognitive framework which they themselves have chosen. Apart from the specialists who are themselves believers and bring their Jewish or Christian theological culture to bear on the question at hand, all who declare themselves agnostic, atheist or simply secular dodge the question of meaning in religious discourse and thus refuse to enter into a discussion of the content of faith, not as a set of life rules to be internalized by every believer, but as a psycho-linguistic social and historical edifice. Hence the essential question about truth, for religious reason as well as that of the most critical philosophical kind, remains totally absent in the so-called scientific study of a corpus of texts of which the raison d'etre – the ultimate goal to which all rhetorical and linguistic utterances bear witness – consists in providing for

its immediate addressees . . . the unique, absolute and intangible criterion of Truth as a True Being, a True Reality and a True Sense of Right.[37]

The Qur'an, like all scriptures, speaks both of its own time and retains authority in our time. Fazlur Rahman (1919–88) was a Pakistani-born scholar who became Professor of Islamic Thought at the University of Chicago. He was one of the first Muslim scholars to stress the urgency of seeing the Qur'an in its Arabian context where the Qur'an is responding to the social and moral environment of seventh-century Arabia. He writes:

If we look at the Qur'an it does not in fact give many general principles: for the most part it gives solutions to the rulings upon specific and concrete historical issues; but as I have said it provides either explicitly or implicitly the rationales behind these solutions and rulings, from which one can deduce general principles. In fact this is the only way to obtain the real truth about the Qur'anic teaching. One must generalize on the basis of Qur'anic treatment of actual cases – taking into due consideration the socio-historical situation then obtaining – since although one can find some general statements of principles there, these for the most part are embedded in concrete treatments of actual issues, whence they must be disengaged.[38]

How is the scholar to approach a text which is both transcendent and immanent? Norman Calder (d.1999), who was a senior lecturer in Islamic Studies at Manchester University, wrote:

For scholars in religious studies, revelation can never be perceived directly as an act of God, or a fact of history.

God's self-revelation to a community can only be accessible to scholarship as a historical process, effectively a literary one, and one in which the community partakes creatively. Irrespective of the degree of metaphor discovered in the notion that God writes himself, it is the writings of God's mediators that are available for analysis. Not even of the Qur'an is it claimed that God dictated, and merely dictated it. God's revelation is not different from the effort of the community to express its understanding of God, and since that (in all its highest forms) is necessarily a literary achievement, it will be subject to the usual conventions of literary type and genre. To know God, it is reading skills that are required. But the act of reading is a creative one: the message depends on the readers' interaction with the text. God is what the reader makes of his (God's) texts.[39]

Muslims must be open to devotional and critical scholarship of the Qur'an. Intellectual engagement with the Qur'an has been a mark of Muslim societies from the very beginning. The Islamic intellectual disciplines of *tafsir* (interpretation), *kalam* (theology) and *fiqh* (law) all bear testimony to this engagement with the Qur'an's language, history and meaning from the earliest period. Academic and scholarly works on the Qur'an continue to pose new challenges for the believer, the believing scholar and the secular scholar. The perception of the Qur'an as a closed book which one can only read, recite and obey, is a problem and fuelled by many Muslims themselves who see any form of critical engagement with the Qur'an as a critique of the Divine, and tantamount to blasphemy. Muslims are forgetting that intellectualism is itself a pious exercise and that faith and intellectualism are not mutually exclusive.

The Muslim world faces many social and ethical problems, caused by changing patterns of Islamic life, migration from Muslim countries to non-Muslim societies and the ethical challenges brought about by living within the framework of secular civil societies. Civil society is based on diversity where different judgements and moralities compete. Furthermore, cultural diversity demands that we compare and contrast value systems and different lifestyles so that we can move together towards building universal values. For many outside the faith, the Muslim world has become synonymous with Muslims burning effigies, shouting anti-Western rhetoric and praising suicide bombers. While many disparate voices attempt to distance Islam from such images, there are many who remain defiant, indifferent to how Islam is being represented and how their discourse is turning the faith into a danger threatening the Western world. They yearn for the glories of a dominant Muslim state in which the transcendent, the material and the political order are intertwined, but often have no concrete sense of what this means in practice. The idealism of this Muslim state makes the dream ever more powerful.

The Qur'an will remain at the heart of Muslim belief and devotion, for it has been sent as a guidance and a mercy for the believer. It will be used to engage in conflict as well as in the pursuit of reconciliation. It will be read and interpreted by believers and non-believers alike. Multi-volume commentaries on the Qur'an have been produced by scholars over centuries for the power of the book lies in its multiple layers of meaning. The faithful will recite it over and over again and they will hear it over and over again. But hearing and reading the Qur'an is only one part of pious reflection. For the Qur'an to continue to speak to the faithful in meaningful ways it must form the basis of an ethics which integrates the

Qur'anic message of justice and compassion within the fullness of human experience. The believer may have to step outside traditional norms of faith and practice and make himself vulnerable to new thinking and new learning. Faith is about openness and humility, not defiant conviction. The earth has been left in man's trust and the burden of this responsibility cannot be overemphasized. If the moral of the creation story places man in a dominant position to other beings, then the earth and its resources are intertwined in a covenant which man has undertaken with God. This covenant extends to our relations with other humans. God's omniscience and majesty remains untouched by what we do, say or write; we can never exhaust his words, but we can reflect God's overriding mercy in more generous readings of our scripture. If we want to draw closer to God, we must respectfully draw closer to each other.

NOTES

1 Daniel Brown, *A New Introduction to Islam*, Blackwell, 2004, p. 10.
2 Patricia Crone, *Meccan Trade and the Rise of Islam*, Princeton University Press, 1987, pp. 149–67.
3 Scholarly opinion claims that the word Qur'an could also have been borrowed from the Syriac *qeryana* which means 'a liturgical reading'.
4 Thus what we have in Ibn Hisham is essentially what Ibn Hisham thought should be preserved from the writings of Ibn Ishaq! This work has been translated into English by Alfred Guillaume under the title, *The Life of Muhammad*, Oxford University Press, USA, 1979.
5 Bukhari's account in *Sahih al-Bukhari*, vol. 1, Book of Revelation, p. 47, Arabic–English translation by Muhammad Muhsin Khan, Darussalam Publications, 1997.
6 Ibid., p. 46.
7 İbrahim Özdemir, 'Environmental Ethics from a Qur'anic Perspective' in Richard Foltz, Frederick Denny and Azizan Baharuddin (eds.) *Islam and Ecology*, Harvard University Press, 2003, p. 7.
8 E. H. Waugh, 'Blood and Blood Clot' in J. D. McAuliffe (ed.) *Encyclopaedia of the Qur'an*, vol. 1, Brill, Leiden 2001, pp. 237–8.
9 For a comprehensive article on this subject, see Aliza Shnizer, 'Sacrality and collection' in Andrew Rippin (ed.), *The Blackwell Companion to the Qur'an*, Blackwell, 2006, pp. 159–71.
10 Ibid., p. 159.
11 These are hadith qudsi 'sacred reports'. I have used Denys Johnson-Davies, *Forty Hadith Qudsi*, The Islamic Texts Society, Cambridge, 1997.

12 This account has been taken from the BBC website, http://newsvote.bbc.co.uk/go/pr/fr/-/2/hi/south_asia/4690338.stm.

13 Fazlur Rahman, *Major Themes of the Qur'an*, Bibliotheca Islamica, Minneapolis, 1980, p. 81.

14 These hadith are from the collection, *An-Nawawi's Forty Hadith*, trans. by Ezzeddin Ibrahim and Denys John-Davies as above.

15 One of the most comprehensive works on women in the Qur'an and medieval commentary is by Barbara Stowasser, *Women in the Qur'an. Traditions and Interpretation*, Oxford University Press Inc., 1994.

16 Thomas Michel, 'Christian Reflections on a Qur'anic Approach to Ecology', full article to be found on http://puffin.creighton.edu/jesuit/dialogue/documents/articles/michel_ecology.htm

17 Sir Muhammad Iqbal, *The Reconstruction of Religious Thought in Islam*, The Ashraf Press, Lahore, 1958, pp. 8–9.

18 William Stoddart, *Sufism*, Delhi, 1983, p. 48.

19 Andrew Rippin, *Muslims*, 3rd ed., Routledge, 2005, p. 103.

20 Frederick Denny, 'Islamic Ritual' in Richard C. Martin (ed.) *Approaches to Islam in Religious Studies*, University of Arizona Press, 1985, p. 66.

21 The Sacred Mosque is considered to be the shrine at Mecca while the Farthest Mosque is Jerusalem. The mosque next to the Dome of the Rock in Jerusalem is called the Farthest Mosque (al-Masjid al-Aqsa).

22 By this I refer to the black full veils of the women and the white pilgrimage clothing of the men, i.e. *ihram*. Although many women come in their own national dress, from a distance it is the black and white image that dominates.

23 In the Judaeo–Christian tradition, it is Isaac not Ishmael.

24 Asma Barlas quoting Fatima Mernissi in 'Women's readings of the Qur'an' in J. D. McAuliffe (ed.), *The Cambridge Companion to the Qur'an*, Cambridge University Press, 2006, p. 257. F. Mernissi, *Women's Rebellion and Islamic Memory*, London, Zed, 1996.

25 It is interesting to note that although this practice is often controlled by men, it is usually women who demand that the practice be enforced.

26 Samuel P. Huntington, 'The Clash of Civilizations', *Foreign Affairs*, vol. 72, no.3, 1993.

27 One of Mernissi's most famous writings is *The Veil and the Male Elite*, trans. by Mary Jo Lakeland, Addison-Wesley, 1991.

28 For an in-depth discussion of this hadith and others, see Khaled Abou el Fadl, *Speaking in God's Name*, Oneworld, Oxford, 2001, pp. 210–18.

29 Al-Bukhari, Muhammad b. Ismail b. al-Mughirah, *Sahih al-Bukhari*, vol. 7, Darrusalam Publishers, Saudi Arabia, 1997, p. 90.

30 Martin Lings, *Muhammad: His Life Based on the Earliest Sources*, London, George Allen and Unwin, 1983, p. 125.

31 The Qur'anic terms for the Hebrew Bible and the Christian Gospels is Tawrat and Injil.

32 M. Sharon, 'People of the Book' in McAuliffe (ed.), *EQ*, vol. 4, pp. 42–3.

33 Mohammad b. Jarir al-Tabari, *Jami' al-bayan 'an ta'wil ay al-Qur'an*, vol. 2, Cairo, Dar al-Ma'rif, 1954, pp. 155–6.

34 The word shari'a originally meant 'path leading to water' or the 'source of life'.

35 A. Kevin Reinhart, 'Jurisprudence' in Rippin, *Blackwell Companion*, p. 447.

36 Omar Bakri Muhammad quoted in 'Attack on London "inevitable."' The full article appeared on 19 April 2004 and can be found on theage.com.au/articles/2004/04/19/1082326119414.html/

37 Mohammad Arkoun, 'Contemporary practices' in McAuliffe (ed.), *EQ*, vol. 1, pp. 413–14.

38 Fazlur Rahman, *Islam and Modernity*, University of Chicago Press, 1982, p. 20.

39 Norman Calder, 'Method and Theory in the Study of Religion', *Journal of the North American Association for the Study of Religion*, 9–1, 1997, Berlin, pp. 47–73.

CHRONOLOGY

The following dates are traditionally cited by scholars as the main dates for when the Qur'an was revealed and the birth and expansion of Islam and Islamic civilization. Most of the dates, however, are approximate. They are all given here in CE

570 Muhammad's date of birth.

595 Marriage of Muhammad and Khadijah.

610 Muhammad receives first revelation from Gabriel.

613 Muhammad begins preaching in Mecca.

619 Death of Muhammad's wife, Khadijah.

622 The Hijra or Muhammad's migration to Medina. The first year of the Islamic calendar.

624 Battle of Badr – Muslims victorious.

625 Battle of Uhud – Muhammad and Muslims defeated by the Meccans.

630 Muhammad occupies Mecca.

632 Death of Muhammad; Abu Bakr becomes first caliph. The beginning of the period of the 'Rightfully Guided Caliphs'.

634 Death of Abu Bakr.

644 Death of Umar, second caliph. Uthman becomes third caliph and the Qur'an is collected and put in codex form during his rule.

656 Death of Uthman, third caliph.

661 Death of Ali, fourth caliph and figurehead of the Shi'i movement.

661–750 Umayyad dynasty – Arab aristocracy.

670 Muslim conquest of northwest Africa.

680–92 Ali's son, Hussein, leads rebellion against the Umayyad caliph Yazid and is martyred.

691 Abd al-Malik completes Dome of the Rock in Jerusalem.

704 Birth of Ibn Ishaq, whose book, in a recension by Ibn Hisham, became one of the most important sources on Muhammad's life.

711 Islam expands into Europe through southern Iberia.

732 Muslims are defeated at the Battle of Tours, halting Islam's expansion further into Europe.

744–50 Defeat of Umayyads by the Abbasids.

750–850 Expansion of Abbasid rule into Egypt, Iran and Syria.

750–1258 Glory of Abbasid rule and Islamic civilization. This period saw the flourishing of the arts, literature, culture, trade and industry. Notable rulers are Harun al-Rashid and al-Mamun.

767 Death of Abu Hanifa, founder of the Hanafi school of law. The Sunni creed, al-Fiqh al-akbar or The Great Fiqh which defines God's unity, is attributed to him.

795 Death of Malik ibn Anas, founder of the Maliki school of law. He compiled one of the most authoritative books of Maliki law, al-Muwatta or 'trodden path', an early collection of hadith.

820 Death of Muhammad al-Shafi'i, founder of Shafii school of law. His most famous work, *Risala* or The Treatise, laid down the principles of Muslim jurisprudence.

855 Death of Ahmed ibn Hanbal, founder of the Hanbali school of law. Hanbalism was revived in Saudi Arabia through the Wahhabi movement and has remained the dominant school of thought in the country.

810–70 Muhammad Bukhari, more commonly known as al-Bukhari, compiled the *Sahih*, regarded by many as the most famous and authentic collection of hadith.

838–923 Muhammad ibn Jarir al-Tabari is considered one of the most prominent Muslim historians and exegetes of the Qur'an. His famous works include *The History of the Prophets and Kings*.

874 Twelfth Shiite Imam goes into occultation or hiding.

874–935 The Muslim theologian al-Ashari becomes the founder of orthodox Sunni kalam.

1058–1111 The period of one of the most celebrated Muslim theologians and philosophers, al-Ghazali. Two of his most famous works are *The Revival of Religious Sciences* and *The Alchemy of Happiness*.

1143 First translation of the Qur'an into Latin.

SUGGESTIONS FOR FURTHER READING

Books on Islam in English vary greatly. From introductory material on Islam and the Qur'an to historical critical studies of early Islam, the literature around Islamic Studies has grown considerably. Most of the general books on Islam have substantial chapters on the Qur'an and Muhammad and can serve as useful introductions to the formation and spread of Islam.

Overview of Islam

One of the most engaging introductory books recently on Islam is Daniel Brown, *A New Introduction to Islam*, Blackwell, 2004.

Frederick Matheson Denny, *An Introduction to Islam*, Macmillan, New York, 1994.

Andrew Rippin, *Muslims: Their Religious Beliefs and Practices*, Routledge, 2005.

An excellent volume of essays and one of the first to bridge the gap between Islamic Studies and the 'methodological richness of the science of religion', is Richard C. Martin (ed.), *Approaches to Islam in Religious Studies*, University of Arizona Press, 1985.

Three notable reference sources for the Qur'an

Jane McAuliffe (ed.), *Encyclopaedia of the Qur'an*, Brill, Leiden, 2001–2006. This is the first multi-volume reference work on the Qur'an in a Western language and an indispensable tool for anyone interested in the Qur'an and Islam.

Andrew Rippin (ed.), *The Blackwell Companion to the Qur'an*, Blackwell, 2006.

Jane McAuliffe, *The Cambridge Companion to the Qur'an*, Cambridge University Press, 2006.

Books on the Qur'an

An accessible English version of the Qur'an is Yusuf Ali, *The Meaning of the Holy Qur'an*, 6th edn., Amana Publications, 1989. It has both the Arabic and English side by side with explanatory material.

An essential reference tool for Islam is *Encyclopaedia of Islam*, 2nd edn., Brill, Leiden, 1960.

A concise but useful guide to the dates and chronology associated with the Qur'an is Ahmad Von Denffer, *Ulum al-Qur'an: An Introduction to the Sciences of the Qur'an*, The Islamic Foundation, Leicester, 1983.

Kenneth Cragg, *The Event of the Qur'an: Islam in its Scripture*, Allen and Unwin, 1971.

For a classic overview of the main themes of the Qur'an by one of the foremost Muslim scholars of Islam, see Fazlur Rahman, *Major Themes of the Qur'an*, Bibliotheca Islamica, Minneapolis, 1980.

Farid Esack, The Qur'an: *A Short Introduction*, Oneworld, 2002.

William Graham, *Beyond the Written Word: Oral Aspects of Scripture in the History of Religion*, Cambridge University Press, 1987.

An excellent analysis of the concept of 'book' in the Qur'an is Daniel Madigan, *The Qur'an's Self-Image*, Princeton University Press, 2001.

Mahmoud Ayoub, *The Qur'an and its Interpreters*, State University of New York Press, 1984.

Muhammad Iqbal, *The Reconstruction of Religious Thought in Islam*, the Ashraf Press, Lahore, 1958.

A provocative book on Western and Islamic methodological approaches to the Qur'an is M. Arkoun, *Rethinking Islam: Common Questions, Uncommon Answers*, trans. by R. D. Lee, Westview Press, Boulder, CO, 1994.

Stefan Wild (ed.), *The Qur'an as Text*, Brill, 1996.

Michael Sells, *Approaching the Qur'an: The Early Revelations*, Ashland, 1999. This book comes with translations of sections of the Qur'an and a CD of recitations.

J. M. S. Baljon, *Modern Muslim Koran Interpretation (1880–1960)*, Brill, Leiden, 1961.

Suha Taji-Farouki (ed.), *Modern Muslim Intellectuals and the Qur'an*, Oxford University Press, 2004.

Jane McAuliffe, *Qur'anic Christians: An Analysis of Classical and Modern Exegesis*, Cambridge University Press, 1991.

Two controversial studies about the emergence of the Qur'an and its historical setting are John Wansbrough, *The Sectarian Milieu: Content and Composition of Islamic Salvation History*, Oxford University Press, 1978, and John Wansbrough, *Qur'anic Studies: Sources and Methods of Scriptural Interpretation*, Oxford University Press, 1977.

Early and Classical Islam

Patricia Crone, *Meccan Trade and the Rise of Islam*, Princeton University Press, 1987.

Chase Robinson, *Islamic Historiography*, Cambridge University Press, 2003.

Wilfred Madelung, *The Succession to Muhammad: A Study of the Early Caliphate*, Cambridge University Press, 1997.

Fred Donner, *Narratives of Islamic Origins*, Darwin Press, 1998.

Michael Cook, *Early Muslim Dogma: A Source Critical Study*, Cambridge University Press, 1981.

Al-Mawardi, *The Ordinances of Government*, trans. by Professor Wafaa H. Wahba, Garnet Publishing, Reading, 1996.

Robert Hoyland (ed.), *Muslims and Others in Early Islamic Society*, Ashgate, 2004.

Richard C. Martin, Mark Woodward and Dwi Atmaja, *Defenders of Reason in Islam: Mutazilim from Medieval School to Modern Symbol*, Oneworld, Oxford, 1997.

Reuven Firestone, *Jihad*, Oxford University Press, 1999

F. E. Peters, Judaism, Christianity and Islam, vol. 1, Princeton University Press, 1990.

Ignaz Goldziher, *Muslim Studies*, 2 vols., Allen and Unwin, 1966, 1971.

Ignaz Goldziher, *Introduction to Islamic Theology and Law*, Princeton University Press, 1981.

Moojan Momen, *An Introduction to Shi'i Islam: the History and Doctrine of Twelver Shiism*, Yale University Press, 1985.

A. J. Wensinck, *The Muslim Creed. Its Genesis and Historical Development*, Cambridge University Press, 1932.

Muhammad Abduh, *The Theology of Unity*, trans. by I. Musàad and K. Cragg, Allen and Unwin, 1966.

Muhammad Sharastani, *Muslim Sects and Divisions*, trans. by A. K. Kazi and J. G. Flynn, Kegan Paul International, 1984.

Sachiko Murata and William C. Chittick, *The Vision of Islam*, I.B.Tauris, London, 1995.

A. J. Arberry, *Sufism: An Account of the Mystics of Islam*, Allen and Unwin, 1950.

Anne-Marie Schimmel, *And Muhammad Is His Messenger: The Veneration of the Prophet in Islamic Piety*, University of North Carolina Press, 1985.

Anne-Marie Schimmel, *Mystical Dimensions of Islam*, University of North Carolina Press, 1975.

Law and Ethics

Norman Calder, *Studies in Early Muslim Jurisprudence*, Clarendon Press, 1993.

Joseph Schacht, *An Introduction to Islamic Law*, Clarendon Press, 1964.

Wael Hallaq, *A History of Islamic Legal Theories*, Cambridge University Press, 1997.

Khaled Abou El Fadl, *Speaking in God's Name*, Oneworld, Oxford, 2003.

Richard G. Hovannisian, *Ethics in Islam*, Undena Publications, Malibu, California, 1985.

Rudolph Peters, *Crime and Punishment in Islamic Law*, Cambridge University Press, 2005.

Yvonne Y. Haddad and Barbara F. Stowasser, *Islamic Law and the Challenges of Modernity*, Altamira Press, CA, 2004.

Jonathan Brockopp (ed.), *Islamic Ethics of Life: Abortion, War, and Euthanasia*, University of South Carolina Press, 1988.

Yohanan Friedmann, *Tolerance and Coercion in Islam*, Cambridge Studies in Islamic Civilization, Cambridge University Press, 2006.

Amyn Sajoo, *Muslim Ethics: Emerging Vistas*, I.B.Tauris, 2004.

Gender and Identity

Abdelwahab Bouhdiba, *Sexuality in Islam*, trans. from the French by Alan Sheridan, Saqi Books, London, 1998.

Ruth Roded (ed.), *Women in Islam and the Middle East*, I.B.Tauris, London, 1999. A useful reader for a wide range of perspectives.

Barbara Stowasser, *Women in the Qur'an: Traditions and Interpretation*, Oxford University Press, 1994. One of the most authoritative and informative works on the Qur'an and women.

Mai Yamani (ed.), *Feminism and Islam*, Ithaca Press, 1996.

Fatima Mernissi, *Beyond the Veil: Male-Female Dynamics in Modern Muslim Society*, Indiana University Press, 1987.

Abdulaziz Sachedina, *The Islamic Roots of Democratic Pluralism*, Oxford University Press, 2001.

Clifford Geertz, *Islam Observed: Religious Development in Morocco and Indonesia*, Yale University Press, 1968.

Leonard Binder, *Islamic Liberalism: A Critique of Development Ideologies*, University of Chicago Press, 1988.

Olivier Roy, *The Failure of Political Islam*, trans. by Carol Volk, I.B.Tauris, 1994.

INDEX